LEADERSHIP STRATEGY

THE ART & SCIENCE OF DECISION-MAKING

POWERFUL BUSINESS SOLUTIONS

INTRODUCTION

"The people who are crazy enough to think they can change the world are the ones who do."

STEVE JOBS

When Apple founder Steve Jobs uttered these iconic words, he perfectly captured the mindset of visionary leaders who profoundly reshape industries, disrupt the status quo, and change the world.

Iconoclasts like Steve Jobs, Jeff Bezos, and Elon Musk possess rare gifts—the ability to envision a radically different future, conceive industry-disrupting ideas, and will them into reality through sheer conviction.

Once seized by a vision of the future, these pioneers align people and resources to execute with precision until their disruptive dreams materialize. They operate in a rare headspace, fixated on possibilities so extraordinary that pragmatists dismiss them as unfounded. But visionaries see latent potential where others don't, and they bend reality to match the future worlds unfolding in their imaginations.

Consider Elon Musk, perhaps an unlikely visionary given his introversion and Asperger's syndrome. Yet Musk has undertaken some of the most ambitious ventures in modern business history. With Tesla, Musk envisioned a future where gasoline cars are replaced by stylish, high-performance electric vehicles. Tesla brought this vision to life, catalyzing the electric vehicle revolution.

Meanwhile, Musk's SpaceX aims to make humanity an interplanetary species by colonizing Mars with rapidly reusable rockets. SpaceX has slashed the cost of spaceflight by 90% while reviving public excitement for space exploration.

Musk believes being a visionary is about perceiving an incredible future and devoting yourself fully to making it real. His vaulting ambition and resolve in the face of skeptics animates his success.

Similarly, Steve Jobs operated lightyears ahead of trends. He co-founded Apple in 1976 with a vision to make complex computing accessible through elegantly simple design. Though ousted from Apple in 1985, Jobs actualized his vision upon returning in 1997, disrupting music, phones, and more with innovations like the iMac, iPod, iPhone, and iPad.

As Jobs remarked, "Innovation distinguishes between a leader and a follower." Realizing a bold vision requires trailblazing new paths rather than following convention. Visionaries like Jobs and Musk thrive on this.

This book reveals how iconoclasts like Jobs, Musk, and other pioneering visionaries cultivate the rare capabilities empowering them to transform entire industries. It examines the mental frameworks, leadership approaches, and innovative strategies they employ to change the world.

We will explore facets of visionary leadership, including:

- **Thinking in Transformational Time Frames:** Visionaries like Musk and Bezos think in timeframes of decades, not quarters. Their ambitions seem unfounded only because pragmatic executives underestimate long-term possibilities. Thinking exponentially expands what visionaries deem achievable.
- **Perceiving Possibilities Early:** Visionaries detect hints of the future well before trends emerge. Steve Jobs glimpsed mobile computing long before smartphones. Jeff Bezos saw the potential of Internet commerce when most dismissed it. Spotting patterns early lets visionaries make calculated bets.
- **Challenging Orthodoxy:** Visionaries stay open to ideas that clash with conventional wisdom.

Rather than accept "how things are done," they ask "why?" Musk challenged assumptions that rockets are necessarily expendable. Jobs saw no reason computers needed command-line interfaces. This willingness to reexamine orthodoxy unlocks creative breakthroughs.

- **Cultivating Extraordinary Courage:** Pursuing disruptive visions requires resilience against constant uncertainty, doubt, and criticism. Visionaries remain committed despite high probabilities of failure. They endure setbacks while never losing sight of their goal. For them, quitting is not an option. Their courage stems from intense conviction.

- **Strategies for Industry-Shaking Innovation:** Visionaries don't just speculate; they strategize. They assemble the elements needed to translate imagination into disruptive innovations, from funding to talent to operational models. Design excellence, leveraging new technologies, and setting audacious goals all drive visionary thinking.

- **Building Visionary Organizations:** Visionaries build uniquely innovative cultures, avoiding bureaucracy and groupthink. They favor flat structures with information flowing freely. Visionaries empower decentralized teams and cultivate diversity of thought. Data, experimentation, and grassroots initiative take priority over hierarchy and convention.

- **Executing Visions Flawlessly:** Converting imagination into reality requires flawless execution. Visionaries create detailed roadmaps to outrageously ambitious goals and then focus ruthlessly on each milestone. They double down when proven right but adjust tactics fluidly when flaws emerge. Their sense of urgency never wavers.

- **Sustaining an Enduring Legacy:** Visionaries embed their principles into organizations, spurring entire new industries. The vision to popularize electric vehicles or space travel accelerates humanity's potential. And their accomplishments compel new generations of visionaries to aim even higher.

This book provides an inside look at how epoch-defining visionaries like Jobs, Musk, and Bezos operate. By examining their mental frameworks, leadership styles, and innovation strategies, we can distill timeless lessons for igniting our own visionary capabilities.

Visionaries reject limiting constraints, seeing infinite human possibility. We all have dormant visionaries within us. This book provides the blueprint for bringing them to life and leading disruptive change. The future favors the bold—are you ready to reimagine what's possible?

CHAPTER 1
CULTIVATING A
VISIONARY MINDSET

IN A WORLD that often celebrates incremental improvements and steady progress, the ability to identify and seize transformational opportunities sets visionary leaders apart. These unique individuals don't just make things better; they redefine what's possible, turning the unthinkable into reality. This chapter explores the thought patterns and insights that enable such visionaries to envision and capture transformational opportunities, transcending the boundaries of conventional thinking.

Take the case of Reed Hastings, the co-founder of Netflix. In the late 1990s, Hastings envisioned a seismic shift in how people accessed and consumed media. At a time when video rental stores dominated and the concept of streaming digital content was a distant possibility, he recognized an opportunity to revolutionize the entertainment industry. Hastings' thought patterns diverged significantly from the norm. While most were focused on optimizing the existing video rental model, Hastings was contemplating a future where physical media would become obsolete. He foresaw a world where convenience, personalization, and instant access would drive consumer preferences.

What set Hastings apart was his ability to perceive not just the limitations of the current model but the latent potential of emerging technologies. His foresight was underpinned by an unwavering belief in the power of the Internet long before high-speed internet became ubiquitous. Hastings did not limit his thinking to the 'how' of the present; he was consumed by the 'what if' of the future. This ability to envision a radically different future and his willingness to act on this vision despite uncertainty and skepticism is the hallmark of a visionary leader.

In this chapter, we're going to unpack the thought processes that underlie such remarkable foresight and innovation as seen in leaders like Reed Hastings. We'll dissect how these visionaries approach opportunities differently, their knack for impeccable timing, and their willingness to embrace risk for the sake of transformative change. This chapter is about enabling you to spot and leverage transformative opportunities in your own professional sphere.

EXPANSIVE FUTURE THINKING

Expansive future thinking is a key trait among visionary leaders. This approach marks a clear departure from the conventional, linear thinking that dominates much of the business world. While linear thinking revolves around gradual improvements, sequential progress, and a predictable trajectory, expansive future thinking steps out of this box. It adopts a broader, more imaginative view, focusing on long-term possibilities and holistic perspectives. This kind of thinking is less about following a set path and more about envisioning a range of potential futures and the paths to reach them.

Expansive future thinking involves looking beyond the immediate horizon and considering a wider array of possibilities, many of which may seem implausible or distant at first glance. It's about understanding that the future is not a linear extension of the present but a landscape of multiple, often unpredictable, pathways. Visionaries like Jeff Bezos and Elon Musk exemplify this thinking. They do not merely anticipate the next step in their industry's evolution; they imagine what the next leap could be, even if it seems disconnected from the current reality.

This type of thinking requires a certain comfort with ambiguity and uncertainty. Unlike linear thinking, which often seeks to minimize risk and focus on incremental gains, expansive future thinking embraces the unknown. It involves asking 'What if?' questions that challenge the status quo and exploring scenarios that others might dismiss as fanciful or irrelevant. For instance, before electric cars became mainstream, asking, "What if cars could be powered entirely by electricity and still outperform traditional vehicles?" would have seemed like wishful thinking. Yet, this 'what if' scenario laid the groundwork for the revolutionary impact of companies like Tesla.

Moreover, expansive future thinking is inherently interdisciplinary. It draws from diverse fields and perspectives, understanding that breakthroughs often occur at the intersection of different disciplines. This approach contrasts with the siloed, specialized focus of traditional linear thinking. By integrating insights from technology, sociology, economics, and environmental science, for example, visionaries can develop a more comprehensive view of future possibilities.

Let's move on to explore how you can develop and nurture this expansive way of thinking. The journey involves training your mind to focus on possibilities instead of limitations, encouraging you to think beyond the traditional confines of your field. Embracing interdisciplinary thinking is crucial here, as it allows you to blend different perspectives and insights. Additionally, you'll learn to systematically question and challenge the underlying assumptions of current business models. This is not just about foreseeing what the future holds; it's about actively shaping and creating that future. By mastering this mindset, you'll equip yourself to not only anticipate change but to drive it.

CHALLENGING ASSUMPTIONS IN YOUR FIELD

Challenging assumptions within your industry is a cornerstone of visionary leadership, serving as a catalyst for innovation and transformative change. Every industry operates on a set of underlying assumptions, often unexamined, that dictate how businesses function and compete. Futuristic strategists distinguish themselves by questioning these deeply ingrained beliefs, thereby unlocking new avenues for groundbreaking ideas and solutions.

To challenge assumptions effectively, one must first identify them. These assumptions can be about consumer behavior, technological limitations, business models, or market dynamics. For example, the assumption in the automotive industry was that vehicles must be powered by internal combustion engines. Electric vehicles (EVs) were seen as impractical due to perceived limitations in range and performance. However, visionaries like Elon Musk challenged this assumption, leading to the rise of high-performance EVs and a redefinition of what cars could be.

Challenging assumptions requires a blend of critical and creative thinking. It involves asking probing questions like, "Why is this the accepted way of doing things?" "What if the opposite were true?" "What are we overlooking?" This line of inquiry can reveal blind spots in traditional thinking and open up previously unexplored opportunities.

Another aspect of challenging assumptions is the willingness to experiment and learn from failures. Innovative ideas often arise from trial and error, and a willingness to take calculated risks. For instance, the assumption in retail was that people prefer to shop in physical stores. Companies like Amazon challenged this notion, experimenting with online retail models that many initially doubted. Their success has not only transformed retail but also altered consumer expectations globally.

RE-IMAGINING SYSTEMS AND PROCESSES

Let's consider the healthcare industry as an example. Traditionally, healthcare systems have been centered around reactive care, where treatment is provided after a person falls ill. However, a visionary approach would be to re-imagine this system with a focus on preventative care. This could involve integrating advanced data analytics, wearable health monitoring devices, and AI-powered diagnostics to predict and prevent illnesses before they occur. Such a shift not only improves patient outcomes but also reduces the overall cost and burden on healthcare systems.

Re-imagining systems requires a deep understanding of the current processes but also an ability to detach from them. It involves asking questions like, "If we were to start from scratch, how would we design this system?" or "What if we could remove existing barriers or limitations?" By doing this, visionaries can identify inefficiencies, redundant steps, or outdated practices that are ripe for innovation.

In addition to ideation, re-imagining systems also requires a holistic view. It's not just about changing one part of the system but understanding how all parts interconnect and influence each other. For instance, re-imagining the education system isn't just about introducing new technology in classrooms. It also involves rethinking teaching methodologies, assessment systems, and even the physical layout of educational institutions to create an environment that fosters holistic learning and creativity.

PIONEERING NEW FRONTIERS

Visionary innovators are also willing to pioneer new frontiers. This aspect of a visionary mindset involves venturing into uncharted territories, whether it be unexplored markets, emerging technologies, or novel business models. It's about identifying and seizing opportunities that others haven't yet seen or considered possible.

A quintessential example of a leader who pioneered a new frontier is Sir Richard Branson with his venture, Virgin Galactic. Branson's foray into commercial space travel exemplifies how visionary leaders are not just innovators but also explorers. In the early 2000s, space travel was largely the domain of government agencies like NASA. However, Branson saw an opportunity in commercial space tourism, a concept that was nearly science fiction at the time. His vision was to make space accessible to private citizens, thereby opening a completely new market.

What motivated Branson was not just the potential for financial gain but a genuine passion for exploration and a belief in the progress of humanity? He was driven by the dream of creating something truly revolutionary and leaving a lasting impact. This intrinsic motivation is a common trait among visionaries who pioneer new frontiers. They are often driven by a deep-seated desire to break barriers, change paradigms, and make a significant mark on the world.

The ability to venture into unexplored territories also requires certain enablers. In Branson's case, his previous successes with the Virgin Group provided the financial resources and business acumen necessary to embark on such a risky venture. Moreover, his willingness to collaborate with experts in aerospace and his ability to inspire and rally a team around his vision were crucial. This highlights that pioneering new frontiers often involves a blend of personal passion, strategic resource allocation, and collaborative effort.

DEVELOPING MENTAL FLEXIBILITY

Mental flexibility and adaptability are two key attributes of a visionary leader. Mental flexibility refers to the ability to shift thinking and adapt to new, evolving, or complex situations. It's a critical skill for navigating the uncertainties and rapid changes characteristic of today's business environment.

Developing mental flexibility is a critical aspect of visionary leadership, and there are several practices and exercises that leaders can adopt to enhance this skill. Engaging in scenario planning, for instance, where you imagine various future scenarios, including unlikely ones, prepares you to handle a range of possibilities and trains your mind to be more flexible. Similarly, using mind maps for brainstorming helps in visualizing problems and solutions, fostering non-linear thinking, and the exploration of multiple facets of a situation.

Exposing yourself to diverse ideas and perspectives is also key. This could be through reading books outside your field, attending workshops on new subjects, or interacting with people from varied backgrounds. Such diverse exposure inevitably leads to more flexible thinking. Complementing this with reflection and journaling can offer deep insights into your thought processes and areas for increased adaptability.

Practicing cognitive flexibility through activities that require quick switching between tasks, like brain training games or improvisational exercises, can significantly improve your mental agility. Moreover, incorporating mindfulness and meditation practices enhances your ability to remain present and adaptable in changing circumstances. Participating in role-playing scenarios and simulation exercises can further hone your ability to think quickly and understand various perspectives.

Regular feedback mechanisms are vital too, as they provide new insights and help in adjusting your approach more flexibly. Embracing failures as learning opportunities fosters a mindset conducive to experimentation and risk-taking, both essential for developing mental flexibility. Additionally, working on cross-functional projects with teams from different departments broadens your perspective, enhancing your adaptive thinking skills.

Incorporating these practices into your daily routine will not only develop your mental agility but also prepare you for visionary leadership. This agility plays a crucial role in fostering another key trait in visionary leaders: curiosity. Cultivating curiosity in leadership involves an eagerness to learn, explore, and question the status quo, setting the stage for innovation and transformative change.

CULTIVATING CURIOSITY IN LEADERSHIP

Curiosity, with its inherent tendency to make us delve deeper and understand the world around us, acts as a formidable force in driving visionary leadership. It fuels leaders to challenge existing norms, constantly seek fresh knowledge, and venture into new, unexplored areas. In this section, we'll delve into various strategies that leaders can employ to foster this sense of curiosity, both within themselves and among their team members.

Fostering an environment that prioritizes continuous learning and skill development is essential. This might mean providing your team with access to various training programs, workshops, or educational resources. It's important to encourage them to expand their knowledge beyond their immediate areas of expertise, which helps in broadening their perspectives.

Another key aspect is promoting a culture that values the art of asking questions. Encourage your team to regularly engage in queries like 'why,' 'what if,' and 'how might we.' This practice not only stimulates curiosity but can also pave the way for innovative solutions and fresh ideas.

Additionally, it's beneficial to expose both yourself and your team to a wide range of experiences, cultures, and viewpoints. This could take the form of working with cross-functional teams, attending industry conferences, or bringing in guest speakers from diverse fields. Such varied experiences are invaluable in igniting new ideas and bringing in different perspectives.

Regularly conducting brainstorming sessions where every idea is welcomed and valued is a great way to encourage creative thinking. This practice not only fosters an atmosphere where exploration and curiosity are celebrated but also opens up a platform for diverse thoughts and innovations.

As a leader, it's also crucial to lead by example in

showcasing curiosity. Share your learning journey, ask insightful questions, and display genuine enthusiasm for new ideas. When you, as a leader, demonstrate curiosity, it sets a positive precedent for the rest of the organization, encouraging others to follow suit.

Another important aspect is to create an environment where experimentation is encouraged, and failure is seen as a part of the learning process. Allowing your team the freedom to experiment and learn from their failures can significantly enhance curiosity and foster a culture of innovative thinking. This approach helps in developing a resilient and adaptable team, ready to tackle challenges with a fresh perspective.

Allocating regular time for both yourself and your team to engage in creative thinking is crucial. This time should be free from the pressures of immediate tasks or looming deadlines, allowing space for individual reflection or group discussions about potential future scenarios or opportunities. Such periods dedicated to creativity can spark innovative ideas and strategies.

In setting goals, try adopting a curiosity-driven approach. Rather than basing goals solely on current knowledge and capabilities, include some objectives that necessitate learning and exploration. This method can be a powerful motivator for your team, encouraging them to acquire new knowledge and skills and to venture beyond their comfort zones. This kind of goal-setting not only pushes the boundaries of what's currently achievable but also fosters a culture of continuous growth and learning.

Encourage your team to stay informed not only about trends and developments within your industry but also in other fields. This broader awareness is key to identifying potential opportunities and threats early on. Keeping abreast of a wide range of topics can provide new insights and ideas that could be beneficial for your business.

Additionally, it's beneficial to work with your team members to develop personal development plans that focus on exploration and learning. These plans should be tailored to each individual's interests and career goals, incorporating chances to delve into new areas and expand their horizons.

By actively cultivating curiosity, leaders can create an environment where constant learning and innovation are part of the organizational culture. This approach not only enhances individual growth but also contributes significantly to the overall progress and adaptability of the team.

FROM INCREMENTAL TO TRANSFORMATIONAL

Trailblazing innovators also go beyond incremental improvement to truly transformational change. This shift is fundamental to the visionary mindset. Incremental improvement involves making small, continuous changes or enhancements to existing products, services, or processes. It's about doing things better. In contrast, transformational change is about doing things differently —it involves rethinking and radically altering the existing state of affairs to create something entirely new and groundbreaking.

Understanding the distinction between incremental and transformational change is critical. Incremental change typically involves predictable and safe improvements, focusing on optimizing and refining existing processes or products. On the other hand, transformational change is much more disruptive and bold. It often requires a complete overhaul of the existing system or an entirely novel approach to a problem or opportunity.

Visionaries often focus on transformational change because of their desire to make a significant impact. They are not satisfied with just making minor improvements to the status quo. Instead, they are driven by the ambition to create something revolutionary —to change the game entirely. This ambition is rooted in a belief that it's possible to make substantial, meaningful differences, going far beyond mere incremental adjustments.

Transformational change, while more risky due to its disruptive nature, also brings with it greater rewards. The risks are often offset by the potential to create new markets, establish significant competitive advantages, and even redefine entire industries. This kind of change doesn't just alter the way we do things; it can change the very fabric of an industry.

However, it's also crucial to balance this with the

value of incremental improvements. The most effective strategies typically combine both approaches. This blend ensures steady, continuous progress while simultaneously making room for those game-changing innovations that can propel an organization forward. In pursuing this balance, leaders must also be mindful of overcoming cognitive biases, which can affect decision-making and impede the successful implementation of both incremental and transformational changes.

OVERCOMING COGNITIVE BIASES

A critical step for visionary leaders is overcoming cognitive biases. Cognitive biases are systematic patterns of thinking errors that result in systematic deviations from rationality. Leaders who are susceptible to cognitive biases find it challenging to make accurate and objective judgments. They can have difficulty identifying and removing sources of bias, leading to poor decision-making and hindering transformational change.

Overcoming cognitive biases is crucial for visionary leadership, and there are several important tips to help in this process. First, it's vital to evaluate your own beliefs and attitudes. Conducting a self-assessment to identify any personal biases is essential for clear judgment. Then, make sure to seek diverse perspectives. Consulting with a wide range of sources and gathering insights from different stakeholders and experts can provide a more rounded view of any situation.

It's also important not to seek out only those opinions that confirm your existing beliefs or biases. Instead, actively look for viewpoints that challenge your preconceptions. Along with this, regularly challenge your own assumptions. Ask yourself whether the assumptions you've made are truly valid. Finally, before implementing any ideas or solutions, make sure to test and validate them thoroughly. This helps in ensuring that your decisions are not clouded by biases.

By recognizing and actively addressing cognitive biases, visionary leaders can make decisions that are more objective and strategic, thereby accelerating the process of transformational change.

HARNESSING DIVERGENT THINKING

Divergent thinking is all about letting your mind explore a whole bunch of different solutions to come up with creative ideas. For visionary leaders, this way of thinking is super important. It's like breaking out of the usual way of thinking and seeing things from new angles. This helps in spotting those big, game-changing opportunities and coming up with really innovative ideas that can make a real difference.

TECHNIQUES FOR ENGAGING IN DIVERGENT THINKING:

When it comes to engaging in divergent thinking, there are a few fun and creative techniques you can use. First up, why not try some brainstorming sessions? In these sessions, let everyone throw in their ideas, no matter how out-of-the-box they seem, and hold off on any judgment. It's all about letting the ideas flow freely and seeing what sticks.

Then, there's mind mapping. This is a cool way to visually lay out your thoughts, showing how different ideas and concepts connect with each other. It's great because it gets you thinking in a non-linear way, which can really open up new perspectives on a problem or situation.

Another neat trick is the SCAMPER technique. It stands for Substitute, Combine, Adapt, Modify, Put to another use, Eliminate, and Reverse. You take an existing product, service, or strategy and mess around with it using these prompts. It's a fantastic way to give old ideas a fresh twist and come up with something completely new.

Another great method to spur divergent thinking is the Six Thinking Hats approach, developed by Edward de Bono. This method gets you to look at problems from various angles—like emotional, informational, analytical, and creative perspectives. It's like putting on different hats to see the world in a new light.

Then there's reverse thinking. It's kind of like doing a mental backflip—instead of the usual problem-to-solution route, you start with the end goal and work your way backward to figure out the steps to get there. This approach can really open up new pathways of thought.

Role-playing exercises are also super helpful. Have your team members step into different roles or personas. This switch-up can lead to some surprising new insights and really get those creative juices flowing.

Lastly, try encouraging analogical thinking. This is all about making connections between things that don't seem related at first glance. By drawing parallels between different domains or industries, you can stumble upon some really unique ideas and solutions.

Regularly challenging the existing assumptions within your industry or organization is a crucial practice. Encourage yourself and your team to question the status quo by asking, "What if we did the opposite?" or "What if this constraint were removed?" This kind of questioning can open up new avenues for innovation and problem-solving.

Introducing creative constraints can also be a surprisingly effective way to spark creativity. By imposing artificial limitations or unique challenges, you often compel people to think outside the box and come up with more creative solutions than they might under normal circumstances.

Lastly, ensuring that team members are exposed to a variety of experiences is key. Encourage them to interact with different cultures, disciplines, and industries. This exposure to diverse ways of thinking not only broadens their horizons but also inspires new ideas and approaches, which is invaluable in a dynamic business environment.

IDENTIFYING TRANSFORMATIONAL OPPORTUNITIES:

Divergent thinking plays a critical role in expanding the pool of ideas and solutions that are considered. This broadening of perspectives significantly increases the chances of identifying truly innovative and transformational opportunities. By stepping outside the usual confines of thought, leaders can uncover a wider array of potential paths and solutions.

This approach also involves breaking away from conventional boundaries. When leaders move beyond linear and traditional ways of thinking, they open the door to unconventional solutions. These fresh, out-of-the-box ideas have the potential not just to improve existing markets and industries but to revolutionize them or even create entirely new ones.

Furthermore, divergent thinking encourages a culture of calculated risk-taking and innovation. Embracing this mindset is essential for driving transformative change. It creates an environment where taking risks and innovating aren't just accepted; they're expected, laying the groundwork for significant breakthroughs and advancements.

Embracing divergent thinking is key to enhancing problem-solving skills in business. This approach involves considering challenges from multiple perspectives, leading to more well-rounded and innovative solutions. By encouraging a look beyond the immediate and obvious, it opens the door to more complex and creative problem-solving. This not only results in stronger solutions but also nurtures a more robust and inventive approach to challenges.

Additionally, divergent thinking fosters cognitive flexibility and adaptability, crucial traits in today's rapidly changing business world. It trains the mind to quickly adapt to new environments and to pivot strategies efficiently when needed. Harnessing this form of thinking allows leaders to create a dynamic environment that nurtures transformational ideas, paving the way for significant advancements and disruptive innovations. This strategic approach positions organizations not just to keep pace but to lead in their respective industries.

BUILDING A VISIONARY CULTURE

Fostering a visionary culture within an organization is pivotal for leaders aiming to cultivate an environment that supports innovative thinking and challenges the status quo. A visionary culture encourages employees to think beyond conventional boundaries and embrace transformational change. Here's how leaders can build such a culture:

STRATEGIES FOR FOSTERING A VISIONARY CULTURE:

To foster a visionary culture, leaders must lead by example, showcasing the innovative thinking, risk-taking, and commitment to transformative change they wish to see in their organization. Creating a safe environment where employees feel comfortable taking calculated risks is also essential. This means viewing failures as learning opportunities, which promotes a culture of experimentation and innovation.

Additionally, promoting open communication is crucial. Establishing an environment where ideas and feedback are freely exchanged across all levels enhances transparency, fosters the sharing of visionary ideas, and facilitates collaborative problem-solving. This open dialogue is key to nurturing a forward-thinking culture.

Fostering a visionary culture also involves actively valuing diverse perspectives within your team. Embracing a variety of viewpoints and experiences not only leads to more innovative solutions but also challenges the status quo. Additionally, investing in the continuous learning and development of employees is crucial. Providing access to workshops, seminars, and training sessions focused on creative thinking, innovation, and current industry trends is key to nurturing a forward-thinking mindset.

Furthermore, recognizing and rewarding innovative ideas and solutions is vital. By acknowledging and incentivizing employees who think creatively and contribute ambitively, you foster an environment that encourages innovation and bold thinking. This recognition serves as a strong motivator, driving the team to continually push boundaries and think outside the box.

To further cultivate a visionary culture, it's important

to foster collaborative ideation. Implementing platforms or holding regular meetings for brainstorming where employees can collectively develop ideas often leads to more innovative and robust outcomes. Setting ambitious, long-term goals that challenge the existing norms is also crucial. These goals should inspire employees to think big and push the limits of what's possible.

Encouraging interdisciplinary learning is another key strategy. Breaking down organizational silos and promoting cross-functional collaboration opens up opportunities for new ideas and approaches, drawing from diverse fields and disciplines. Additionally, investing in innovative tools and technologies equips employees with the resources they need for creative thinking and experimentation, further driving the culture of innovation and forward-thinking.

Cultivating a customer-centric mindset is essential in fostering a visionary culture. Encourage employees to consistently consider the customer's perspective, emphasizing the creation of value and solving real-world problems. This approach not only leads to higher engagement among team members but also fuels their motivation to innovate.

Additionally, it's important to regularly review and adapt organizational processes to ensure they promote innovative thinking and efficiency. This means avoiding rigid routines that can stifle creativity and instead maintaining a dynamic environment where processes are continually evolved to foster a culture of continuous improvement and innovation.

By implementing these strategies, leaders can build a culture that not only supports but champions visionary thinking, laying the groundwork for transformative success and innovation within the organization.

CHAPTER 2

THE COURAGE TO PURSUE BOLD VISIONS

VISIONARY LEADERS ARE RENOWNED for their bold decisions and groundbreaking achievements. At the heart of these accomplishments lies not just risk-taking but the skill to discern and take smart risks. The nuanced distinction between smart risks and reckless moves is a critical aspect of visionary leadership. Understanding how these leaders assess and decide which risks are worth taking is key to understanding their success.

UNDERSTANDING SMART RISKS VERSUS RECKLESS MOVES

Visionary leadership hinges on smart risk-taking, where decisions are calculated and aligned with the leader's vision and goals. Smart risks involve in-depth research and careful consideration of outcomes, unlike reckless moves that are often impulsive and lack thorough assessment. Visionary innovators distinguish themselves by systematically evaluating risks, understanding that the process of assessment is as vital as the decision to take the risk itself.

When visionary leaders assess risks, their first step is to check how the risk aligns with their overall vision and long-term objectives. They carefully consider whether the risk will bring them closer to their goals or detract from their focus. To understand the potential impact of the risk, they gather extensive information and insights, relying on data, research, and expert opinions.

A crucial part of this process is evaluating the pros and cons of the risk. Leaders meticulously analyze both the best-case and worst-case scenarios, taking into account not just the immediate effects but also the long-term implications of their decision. This thorough analysis helps them make informed choices that align with their strategic goals.

Trailblazing innovators understand the importance of seeking guidance and different perspectives. Consulting with trusted advisors, such as mentors, peers, and experts, is vital in gaining additional insights, which are crucial for evaluating the feasibility and potential impact of any risk they consider taking.

The timing of their decisions is another key factor. Forward-thinking pioneers meticulously assess market conditions, societal trends, and their organization's readiness before making a move. This careful consideration of timing ensures that their decisions are well-placed and more likely to yield positive results.

Additionally, smart risk-taking for these leaders means being thoroughly prepared for various outcomes. They develop contingency plans to mitigate potential negative effects and remain adaptable, always ready to pivot or adjust their strategies in light of new information or changing circumstances. This level of preparedness and flexibility is a hallmark of their strategic approach to leadership.

RESILIENCE IN THE FACE OF UNCERTAINTY

Visionary leaders maintain direction and motivation even amidst uncertainty by keeping a clear and compelling vision at the forefront. They embrace challenges as opportunities for growth, adopting a mindset that sees uncertainty as a natural part of innovation and approaching it with curiosity. Additionally, emotional resilience is crucial for managing doubt and skepticism. Leaders who practice emotional intelligence and techniques like mindfulness can better handle their emotions and those of their teams, ensuring emotional balance.

Strong leaders recognize the value of a support network comprising mentors, peers, and advisors. This network acts as a sounding board, offers diverse perspectives, and provides strength during challenging times. Visionary leaders also prioritize their physical and mental well-being, understanding that self-care is essential to withstand the demands of leading through uncertainty. Additionally, while they aim high, they set realistic expectations and prepare for setbacks, a strategy that helps manage stress and prevents disillusionment when encountering obstacles.

Adaptability and agility are hallmarks of resilient leadership. Visionary leaders excel in adapting and pivoting in response to changing circumstances, continually reassessing situations, and adjusting their strategies as necessary. They also draw strength from their past experiences, including failures, using these to gain insights, refine strategies, and strengthen their resolve. Furthermore, patience and persistence are essential, especially when facing skepticism or slow progress. Visionary leaders recognize that meaningful change takes time and that consistent persistence is crucial for overcoming challenges and achieving long-term goals.

COMMITMENT DESPITE FAILURES AND CRITICISM

Visionary innovators have an unwavering conviction and commitment, even in the face of uncertainty and challenges. They are deeply aware of their purpose and the reasons behind their goals, which act as a guiding compass through daunting times. Their passion and commitment to their work and ambitions drive them, fueling their resolve in the face of obstacles. Moreover, they understand the importance of resilience and perseverance, embracing failures and setbacks as part of the journey. These experiences don't deter their ambition;

instead, they strengthen their determination to try again and move forward.

Failures and setbacks are crucial learning opportunities. Visionary leaders analyze their failures to glean insights and lessons, which then equip them to navigate similar challenges in the future more effectively. In addition to this learning-oriented approach, they also possess a strong sense of personal values and principles, remaining steadfast to these core beliefs even in the face of criticism and skepticism. Practicing mindfulness helps them stay grounded and present, an essential trait, particularly when under pressure or stress. This mindfulness not only aids in maintaining focus but also in making well-considered decisions.

Futuristic strategists recognize the importance of collaboration and teamwork. They actively seek support from mentors, advisors, and collaborators who can assist them in overcoming obstacles and making informed decisions. These leaders also maintain a hopeful and optimistic outlook toward the future, even in challenging times, trusting that their efforts will ultimately bear fruit. Additionally, their drive for excellence and quality in their work keeps them focused and undeterred by criticism or skepticism. Motivated by self-improvement and a deep passion for their work, they consistently aim to raise the bar in their endeavors.

Trailblazing innovators understand the transformative power of time and are open to growth and evolution. They acknowledge that their methods and approaches might need to adapt over time, informed by new experiences and information. Such adaptability and willingness to evolve form the cornerstone of visionary leadership. These strategies and mindsets are fundamental in enabling leaders to persevere through failures, skepticism, and the various risks and uncertainties that come with the territory of transforming industries and challenging the status quo.

EMOTIONAL INTELLIGENCE IN VISIONARY LEADERSHIP

Emotional intelligence plays a crucial role in visionary leadership. It is the ability to understand and regulate emotions, both one's own and those of others. It is the basis for building positive relationships, fostering collaboration, and making strategic decisions.

The role of emotional intelligence in visionary leadership cannot be overstated. It equips leaders with the ability to understand not only their own emotions but also those of others. This understanding is crucial in navigating tense situations with empathy and compassion, which in turn helps in building trust and rapport. Visionary leaders with high emotional intelligence are adept at managing stress and maintaining calm and control, even in challenging circumstances. This ability to stay composed is essential in leading effectively through turbulent times.

Moreover, emotional intelligence is a key factor in developing trusting and collaborative relationships within teams. Visionary leaders use their emotional intelligence to communicate clearly and empathize with team members, creating an environment of cooperation and mutual support. This cultivates a positive team culture, where members feel valued and understood, further strengthening the team's collective ability to achieve their goals.

Emotional intelligence is a cornerstone of visionary leadership, playing a vital role in various aspects of leadership. It allows leaders to objectively evaluate decisions and options, steering clear of biases and emotional blind spots. An emotionally intelligent leader is adaptable and flexible, capable of pivoting and adjusting their strategies as needed.

Such leaders are also more effective in motivating and inspiring their teams, connecting with team members emotionally to foster a sense of shared purpose and commitment. They are adept at handling conflicts and maintaining composure even in tense situations. Moreover, emotional intelligence is key in maintaining a balanced and healthy lifestyle, helping leaders prioritize self-care and prevent burnout, which is crucial for strategic decision-making.

Forward-thinking pioneers with high emotional intelligence understand the power of language and use it effectively to ensure their messages are clear and impactful. They are also skilled at empowering others and fostering an environment conducive to growth and innovation, encouraging team members to excel and enhance their own skills.

MINDFULNESS PRACTICES FOR VISIONARY LEADERS

Mindfulness practices can be an invaluable tool for visionary leaders, helping them maintain focus, manage stress, and recover from setbacks. Here are some essential mindfulness practices:

Visionary innovators can benefit greatly from practices like meditation and breathing exercises, which help maintain a clear and focused mind. Regularly engaging in deep breathing and meditation can foster a sense of calmness and centeredness, even under pressure. Incorporating walking meditation is another effective technique, where focusing on breathing and sensory experiences during a walk can release tension and enhance present-moment awareness.

Mindful eating is another practice that can be beneficial. By paying attention to the taste, texture, and aroma of food, this approach encourages more conscious eating and a deeper appreciation for meals. Physical activities like yoga and tai chi also play a crucial role, combining physical movement with mental focus to relieve stress and improve flexibility, contributing to a calm and centered state of mind.

Journaling and reflection are powerful tools for gaining insights and clarity. They allow leaders to process thoughts, feelings, and experiences, aiding in overcoming challenges. Positive visualization, where one imagines achieving goals and experiencing success, can keep motivation and focus high, especially when facing daunting tasks.

Lastly, self-compassion is essential. Visionary leaders who practice kindness and compassion toward themselves are better equipped to deal with setbacks. Cultivating a self-compassionate mindset aids in resilience and helps maintain drive and focus amidst challenges.

Mindfulness practices can not only aid pioneering leaders in maintaining focus and recovering from setbacks. They can also help them improve their decision-making abilities, strengthen their emotional intelligence, and foster a healthy and balanced lifestyle.

BALANCING CONVICTION WITH ADAPTABILITY

Visionary leaders often face a balancing act between their deep convictions and the need to adapt to new information and changing circumstances. It's essential to strike a balance between these two poles, as too much conviction can lead to stubbornness and blindness, while too much adaptability can lead to compromise and lack of direction.

Pioneering thought leaders can employ several strategies to maintain a balance between conviction and adaptability. One helpful approach is to visualize a set of balancing scales. By metaphorically weighing their convictions against their adaptability, leaders can ensure that neither aspect overshadows the other. This metaphor can guide them in making decisions that are both true to their vision and flexible enough to adapt to changing circumstances.

Prioritizing adaptability is also crucial. While staying committed to their goals and convictions, visionary leaders should remain open to change and willing to pivot when necessary. Being adaptable is key to successfully navigating the uncertainties and evolving landscapes of the business world.

Additionally, listening plays a significant role. Thought leaders benefit from listening to feedback, advice, and insights from various sources, even those they might initially disagree with. This openness to different perspectives can provide valuable new information, helping leaders adjust their approach as the situation demands. This balance of listening—and adapting while staying true to their core beliefs—is essential for effective and visionary leadership.

To successfully navigate complex and rapidly changing situations, innovating leaders need to embrace flexibility. Avoiding too much attachment to a single approach or plan is crucial, as being open to change and adjustment in light of new information is key to effective leadership. This flexibility enables them to respond appropriately to unforeseen challenges and opportunities.

Additionally, celebrating change is important. Change should be viewed as something exciting and inspiring, an opportunity for growth and evolution, rather than something to be feared. Embracing change with enthusiasm can invigorate a team and lead to innovative solutions.

In summary, the ability to strike a balance between conviction and adaptability is a vital skill for visionary leadership. It allows leaders to maintain their focus and direction while also being open-minded and responsive to the dynamic nature of the business world.

LEARNING FROM FAILURES: A VISIONARY APPROACH

Trailblazing leaders are often lauded for their successes and daring goals, yet their ability to learn from failure is just as crucial. They understand that setbacks and failures are opportunities for learning, helping them stay focused, resilient, and strategically savvy. By dissecting the root causes of failures, these leaders can uncover patterns or weaknesses that need addressing, thereby refining their approaches.

For instance, consider the story of Howard Schultz and Starbucks. After stepping down as CEO, Schultz returned to find the company struggling. He embraced the failure, analyzing deeply ingrained attitudes and beliefs within the company that needed change. By owning these failures and fostering a culture of learning and transparency, Schultz turned Starbucks around, reinvigorating its brand and customer experience.

Trailblazing innovators also encourage their teams to

embrace this learning-oriented approach. They share insights from setbacks, fostering a culture of teamwork, collaboration, and mutual learning. Celebrating growth and evolution, not just successes, these leaders maintain a positive outlook, constantly evolving and adapting their strategies.

Staying agile and flexible is key. Visionary leaders are always ready to adjust their approach in response to new information or circumstances, allowing them to navigate through setbacks effectively. They often draw inspiration and motivation from others' stories of overcoming failure, using these tales to fuel their determination and drive.

In essence, learning from failures is a pivotal aspect of visionary leadership. It not only allows leaders to refine their strategies and approaches but also cultivates an environment rich in curiosity, learning, and innovation, setting the stage for breakthrough advancements and disruptive innovations.

CULTIVATING A RESILIENT TEAM CULTURE

Visionary leaders are adept at fostering a resilient team culture that thrives on curiosity, openness, and a willingness to take risks. They focus on building trust and camaraderie, ensuring that communication, collaboration, and mutual support are at the heart of their team dynamics. Recognizing the importance of risk-taking, they reward experimentation and view failures as valuable learning opportunities.

Celebrating successes is just as important as learning from failures for these leaders. They make sure to acknowledge and reward achievements, fostering a positive environment that encourages growth. Additionally, they promote cooperation and co-creation across different functions, creating a sense of shared ownership and investment in the team's endeavors.

Encouraging diverse perspectives through debate and discussion is another strategy they employ, valuing a variety of viewpoints and ideas. Showing gratitude and appreciation not only for results but also for the effort and dedication put in by team members is a key aspect of their leadership style.

Trailblazing innovators also prioritize the development of their teams, offering opportunities that allow for growth and evolution. They strive to keep the work environment enjoyable and energetic, believing that fun and creativity go hand in hand. Challenging assumptions and biases is encouraged to foster critical thinking and thorough analysis.

Establishing clear ground rules and guidelines is another way they provide clarity and direction to their teams. Overall, by creating a resilient team culture, pioneering thought leaders not only pave the way for transformational change but also enhance team morale, build a sense of shared purpose, and cultivate a culture rich in innovation and growth.

CHAPTER 3
MASTERING DISRUPTIVE INNOVATION

IN THE LANDSCAPE of modern business, where incremental improvements often dominate, this chapter delves into the realm of groundbreaking change-makers who go beyond mere optimization to radically transform and redefine industry norms. Here, we will explore the distinctive approaches these leaders employ, their innovative mindsets, and the strategic methodologies that enable them to not just participate in the game but to change it entirely. Join us as we unravel the secrets of mastering disruptive innovation in a world that thirsts for transformative change.

THE MINDSET OF A GAME-CHANGER

The first step in redefining industry standards is adopting a mindset that sees beyond the current limitations and norms. Visionary leaders possess a unique blend of imagination, courage, and foresight that allows them to envision a dramatically different future. This mindset is not constrained by the "this is how we've always done it" mentality. Instead, it is fueled by a deep conviction that change is not only possible but necessary.

STRATEGIES FOR REDEFINING THE GAME

Visionary leaders redefine the game by first questioning and challenging the status quo. They're not afraid to ask 'Why?' and 'What if?' questions that sow the seeds for new ideas and innovations. Their strategies are not just plans but visions of what the industry could become, acting as a north star that guides every decision toward transformative goals.

These leaders embrace radical thinking, entertaining ideas that might initially seem unrealistic or impossible and pushing boundaries to imagine potential futures rather than accepting the present. They build futuristic roadmaps, charting ambitious steps toward their disruptive goals, driven by the very ambition that fuels groundbreaking change.

Understanding and leveraging emerging technologies is another key trait. These leaders stay on top of technological advancements, creatively applying them to disrupt and transform their industry. They're also not shy about taking calculated risks and experimenting with new approaches, resiliently embracing failure as part of the journey.

Equally important is their ability to influence and

persuade stakeholders to buy into their radically different visions. They skillfully convince everyone, from employees to investors, of the value and potential of their transformative ideas.

Furthermore, groundbreaking change-makers create agile and innovative teams, fostering a culture that prizes creativity, flexibility, and a willingness to defy conventional wisdom. A prime example of such a leader is Steve Jobs, co-founder of Apple Inc. Jobs didn't just aim for incremental improvements; he reimagined entire industries, creating products that fundamentally altered human interaction with technology. His approach exemplifies the essence of a visionary leader who changes the game instead of just playing it.

Steve Jobs, together with Steve Wozniak, fundamentally changed personal computing with the introduction of the Apple II, one of the first successful mass-produced personal computers. This innovation wasn't just an improvement on existing technology; it completely redefined personal computers, making them user-friendly and accessible to a wider audience.

In the music industry, Jobs and Apple brought about a transformation with the iPod and iTunes. At a time when the industry was struggling with digital music and piracy, this combination of hardware and software changed the way people bought and consumed music. It shifted the focus from physical CDs to digital downloads, effectively tackling the issue of piracy.

One of Jobs' most groundbreaking contributions was

the iPhone. Before its launch, mobile phones were largely used for calling and texting. The iPhone, with its revolutionary touchscreen interface, app ecosystem, and design emphasis, redefined the smartphone. It set a new standard for what mobile communication could entail, going far beyond just an improvement of existing phones.

Similarly, the iPad marked the creation of the tablet market. Before its introduction, tablet computers were a niche product. The iPad transformed them into mainstream devices, carving out a new category in personal technology that merged the functionalities of a laptop and a smartphone.

In each instance, Steve Jobs didn't merely focus on improving existing products; he completely reimagined them and the entire user experience. His vision was to create products that were not just technologically superior but also intuitive, aesthetically pleasing, and seamlessly integrated into daily life. This approach to innovation led to dramatic changes across multiple industries, including computing, music, and mobile telecommunications, epitomizing what it means to be a visionary leader.

LEVERAGING NEW TECHNOLOGIES AND BUSINESS MODELS TO FLIP INDUSTRY NORMS

Visionary leaders excel in leveraging new technologies and innovative business models to upend traditional industry norms and create significant paradigm shifts.

Their strategies often disrupt established markets, setting new standards in the process. Here's a glimpse into their approach:

These leaders are typically early adopters of emerging technologies, constantly monitoring technological advancements and considering how they can be innovatively applied within their industries. A prime example is Jeff Bezos, who harnessed the early potential of the Internet to create Amazon, revolutionizing the retail industry from traditional brick-and-mortar stores to online shopping platforms.

Another key strategy is reimagining user experience, often in previously unimaginable ways. Apple's launch of the iPhone, for example, was more than the introduction of a new phone. It represented a complete overhaul of the mobile communications user experience with its intuitive touchscreen interface.

Instead of just creating standalone products, visionary leaders often focus on creating ecosystems around their products rather than just releasing standalone items. This approach offers users a more integrated and seamless experience. Google is a standout example, having developed a comprehensive suite of interconnected services and products that address various aspects of digital life. Such ecosystems not only enhance user engagement but also establish a long-lasting market presence.

Leaders like Elon Musk in the automotive sector with Tesla and Reed Hastings with Netflix exemplify how adopting disruptive business models can transform industries. Tesla's innovative direct-to-consumer sales approach and Netflix's subscription-based streaming model have reshaped market dynamics in their respective industries.

Additionally, modern visionary leaders are increasingly focusing on sustainability and ethics within their business practices. This shift is in response to a growing consumer demand for responsible business conduct. Implementing practices such as using renewable energy, ethically sourcing materials, or adopting sustainable manufacturing processes demonstrates a commitment to these values.

The integration of big data analytics and artificial intelligence has also become a critical tool for visionary leaders. This technology provides deep insights into customer behavior, enabling the optimization of operations and the personalization of customer experiences. Amazon's recommendation system stands as a notable example, showcasing how effectively data can be used to enhance the customer experience and boost sales.

Futuristic strategists use agile and lean methodologies to ensure their businesses can swiftly adapt to market changes, enabling them to test and iterate new ideas quickly. This adaptive approach is essential in industries that are in a constant state of evolution.

These leaders are also adept at building scalable solutions that can be easily adapted to various markets and demographics, allowing for rapid expansion and disruption on a global scale. But perhaps their most crucial strategy is fostering a corporate culture that prizes continuous innovation, risk-taking, and forward-thinking. This culture underpins their ability to remain at the forefront of industry evolution.

Overall, visionary leaders redefine industry norms through the strategic use of new technologies and innovative business models. Unafraid to challenge the status quo, they constantly seek ways to innovate and improve, often requiring a comprehensive shift in industry operations. Their success is anchored in their capacity to anticipate future trends, quickly adapt, and effectively execute their visions, thereby shaping the direction of entire industries.

CREATING BLUE OCEAN STRATEGIES IN SATURATED MARKETS

In the business landscape, a "Blue Ocean" represents an untapped market space, in contrast to "Red Oceans," where fierce competition turns the waters bloody. Futuristic strategists excel in identifying and creating these blue ocean opportunities, even in markets that appear entirely saturated. Here's how they achieve this:

Visionary leaders redefine market boundaries by looking beyond established limits to explore new demographics, geographies, and psychographics, often uncovering opportunities missed by competitors. A classic example is Airbnb, which created a new market in the hospitality industry by tapping into the unused personal spaces of homeowners.

They craft innovative value propositions that starkly differentiate their offerings from existing competitors. This often involves combining features traditionally seen as separate or introducing new levels of convenience, experience, or affordability. Another strategy is to disrupt traditional pricing models. Trailblazing innovators might offer more accessible pricing strategies that widen the product or service's appeal, similar to how Netflix revolutionized the video rental market with its subscription model.

Utilizing technology in novel ways is also a key approach, with visionaries often using emerging technologies to create products or services that redefine or establish new consumer behaviors. Moreover, instead of competing for existing customers, they focus on 'noncustomers'—those who have been overlooked or have avoided the market—and tailor their offerings to meet these untapped needs.

Enhancing user experience and design is another path to creating a blue ocean. Products or services that are significantly more user-friendly, enjoyable, or aesthetically pleasing can draw in a new customer base. In the environmentally conscious market of today, focusing on sustainability can also carve out a new niche, as seen with companies like Tesla, where sustainability is a core part of their value proposition.

Building communities or ecosystems around products or services can also be transformative. Apple's ecosystem, integrating various devices and services, exemplifies how this approach can create an entirely new market space. Forming unconventional partnerships and collaborations, which combine different skills, technologies, and insights, can also lead to new market opportunities.

Finally, continuous experimentation and iteration based on customer feedback and rapid prototyping are integral to visionary leadership. This process helps in refining offerings until they open up new market segments, exemplifying the dynamic and innovative nature of creating blue ocean strategies in saturated markets.

In essence, creating blue ocean strategies in saturated markets involves a combination of creativity, foresight, and a willingness to venture beyond conventional wisdom. Visionary leaders excel at understanding latent customer needs, leveraging technology creatively, and thinking beyond the current competitive paradigms to uncover and capitalize on untapped market potential.

THE ART OF CANNIBALIZING YOUR OWN PRODUCTS

Innovation in business often requires making bold moves, one of which is the strategy of cannibalizing your own products. This concept involves a company intentionally introducing new products or services that may adversely affect its existing offerings. Forward-thinking pioneers understand that to stay ahead in a rapidly evolving market, it's sometimes necessary to disrupt their own products before a competitor does. Here's an exploration of why and how they adopt this approach:

UNDERSTANDING PRODUCT CANNIBALIZATION

In fast-paced industries, visionary leaders understand that waiting too long to innovate can allow competitors to surge ahead. To stay at the forefront, they often evolve their own offerings, even if it means overshadowing their existing products. This approach not only keeps them ahead of the competition but also drives continuous innovation within their organizations. It sends a clear message that constant improvement and adaptation to new trends and technologies are top priorities.

Customer needs and preferences are always in flux, and by introducing products that might cannibalize their existing ones, companies ensure they consistently meet or exceed these evolving expectations. An excellent example of this is Apple's introduction of the iPhone, which significantly cannibalized sales of its iPod. This move was a strategic decision to embrace the emerging smartphone technology and meet customers' shifting demands for more integrated mobile devices.

Additionally, as new technologies emerge, they can quickly make previous products outdated. Visionary strategists, therefore, leverage these technological advancements to develop superior products. They recognize that innovating and competing with their previous offerings is essential for long-term success, demonstrating a commitment to staying relevant and leading in their market. This strategy not only sustains their market leadership but also fosters a culture of relentless innovation and adaptability.

FRAMEWORKS FOR PRODUCT CANNIBALIZATION

Visionary leaders engage in thorough market analysis and forecasting to stay ahead of emerging trends and technologies. This foresight helps them predict which products may become obsolete and plan for their successors. A customer-centric approach is crucial; they focus on current and future customer needs rather than relying solely on past successes. This involves actively engaging with customers, gathering feedback, and understanding their changing preferences.

Strategically, they develop innovation roadmaps to plan the introduction of new products while phasing out older ones, ensuring these plans align with the company's overall vision and market trends. Risk assessment is also key. They evaluate the risks of cannibalizing existing products, considering potential revenue loss and customer reactions, and devise strategies like phased rollouts or targeted marketing campaigns to mitigate these risks.

Resource allocation is managed strategically to support new product development while maintaining existing products. This could mean reallocating budgets, talent, and marketing efforts to prioritize innovation. Cross-functional collaboration is another essential element, requiring synchronization across departments like R&D, marketing, and sales for successful product launches.

In some cases, new products may complement rather than replace existing ones, thus expanding the market. Effective communication is vital to explain the reasons for introducing new products that might cannibalize existing ones, both to internal teams and external stake-holders. This transparency helps manage expectations and maintain brand loyalty.

In summary, the strategy of product cannibalization, when implemented with a structured framework, allows companies to stay relevant and competitive. Visionary leaders embrace this approach, understanding the risks but also recognizing the necessity of adapting to market changes, ultimately leading their companies to contin-uous innovation and strengthened market positions.

BUILDING A CULTURE THAT EMBRACES DISRUPTION

Visionary leaders are adept at creating a culture that not only embraces but actively drives disruptive innovation. They recognize the significant influence of an organiza-tion's culture on its capacity to innovate and disrupt. To build such a culture, they focus on several key practices and mindsets.

They cultivate a mindset of openness and curiosity, where questioning the status quo is standard. Encouraging curiosity, open-mindedness, and a willingness to explore new possibilities is vital for identifying opportunities for disruption. Additionally, they foster an environment where employees feel safe to experiment, take risks, and even fail. Promoting a 'fail fast, learn fast' mentality, these leaders view failure as a stepping stone to innovation.

Encouraging cross-disciplinary collaboration is another strategy. Visionary leaders break down silos and bring together cross-functional teams, understanding that a blend of ideas and perspectives can lead to disruptive innovation. They also reward innovation and risk-taking. Recognizing and rewarding employees who come up with new ideas or take calculated risks, even if those ideas don't always succeed, reinforces the value placed on innovation and encourages continuous creative thinking.

Providing continuous learning opportunities is crucial. Visionary leaders invest in developing their team's skills and knowledge, whether through training in new technologies, workshops on creative thinking, or talks by external innovators. This commitment to learning ensures that the team remains at the cutting edge of innovation and disruption.

Leaders who aim to foster a culture of disruption and innovation must lead by example. By visibly challenging industry norms and pioneering new approaches, they can inspire their teams to adopt a similar mindset. Implementing agile methodologies is also key, as it allows for a rapid response to change, encourages quick experimentation, and supports iterative development, all of which are crucial in a culture geared toward innovation.

A clear and compelling vision for change is essential. Visionary leaders articulate this vision to serve as a rallying point for the entire organization, aligning efforts and maintaining focus on the goal of disruption. Customer-centric innovation is also a priority. By consistently focusing on the evolving needs and expectations of customers, organizations can stay ahead of market trends. Leaders encourage their teams to think from the customer's perspective, leading to innovations that are more user-focused.

Instilling a sense of purpose or mission that goes beyond profits and growth is another tactic employed by trailblazing innovators. When teams believe they are working toward something meaningful, their motivation to innovate increases. Utilizing technology as a catalyst for innovation is also critical. Keeping up with technological advancements and understanding their application to current business challenges is key to fostering a disruptive culture.

Lastly, building a diverse and inclusive workforce is fundamental. A variety of thoughts, backgrounds, and experiences contributes to a richer pool of ideas, essential for disruptive innovation. These varied perspectives help in creating solutions that are not only innovative but also inclusive and comprehensive.

Forward-thinking pioneers foster a culture that drives disruptive innovation by encouraging openness, risk-taking, collaboration, and continuous learning. They lead by example, articulate a clear vision, and create an environment where innovative ideas are valued and pursued. This approach not only makes the organization receptive to disruption but also actively cultivates it as a core aspect of its identity.

CHAPTER 4
BUILDING A CULTURE OF INNOVATION

IN THE JOURNEY toward sustained success and impact, fostering a culture of innovation is a critical milestone. This chapter explores the multifaceted approach visionary leaders take to cultivate such a culture within their organizations. It's not just about sparking creativity; it's about nurturing an environment where innovation is the norm, not the exception.

HIRING FOR AN ENTREPRENEURIAL SPIRIT

In building a team that can thrive in a culture of innovation, visionary leaders focus on identifying and attracting individuals with a distinct set of characteristics —those that embody an entrepreneurial spirit. This section of the chapter delves into what these traits are and how visionary leaders recognize them in potential team members.

CHARACTERISTICS OF ENTREPRENEURIAL TEAM MEMBERS

In the world of entrepreneurship, certain characteristics are highly prized in team members, and these traits often set the foundation for innovative and successful ventures. Inherent curiosity is one such trait. Individuals who possess a natural curiosity, constantly seeking to learn and understand the world around them, are invaluable. Their desire to explore new ideas and solutions is a driving force in entrepreneurial endeavors.

Comfort with ambiguity is also crucial in the entrepreneurial landscape, often characterized by uncharted territories. Visionary leaders seek individuals who not only tolerate uncertainty but thrive in it, seeing it as an opportunity for innovation. Alongside this, a propensity for calculated risk-taking paired with the resilience to bounce back from setbacks is essential. These traits indicate an individual's ability to navigate the often turbulent waters of innovation and persevere.

Creative problem-solving is another key characteristic. The ability to think outside the box, especially in challenging situations, is highly valued. Visionary leaders look for team members who can approach problems from unique perspectives and develop innovative solutions. For instance, the team at SpaceX, led by Elon Musk, exemplifies this trait as they tackle the formidable challenge of making space travel more accessible and sustainable.

Proactive and self-driven individuals are also well-suited for entrepreneurial teams. Visionaries appreciate those who can independently drive projects, take ownership of their work, and move initiatives forward without constant oversight. However, despite this strong sense of independence, the ability to collaborate effectively is equally important. Entrepreneurial ventures thrive in environments where team members can work cohesively, share ideas openly, and build on each other's contributions, creating a synergy that drives innovation and growth.

IDENTIFYING AND ATTRACTING THESE INDIVIDUALS

Futuristic strategists tailor their recruitment processes to identify key entrepreneurial traits in candidates. They may employ innovative interviewing techniques, practical problem-solving sessions, or group dynamics assessments to find the right fit. During job postings and interviews, they emphasize the company's mission and vision, attracting individuals who share these values and are excited about contributing to innovation and broader organizational goals.

Creating an appealing company culture is another strategy. A culture that celebrates innovation, creativity, and entrepreneurial thinking naturally draws in like-minded individuals. Leaders make this culture visible to potential hires through various channels like social media, company websites, and during recruitment interactions.

Offering opportunities for growth and learning is also crucial. By highlighting the company's dedication to personal and professional development, they attract candidates looking for continuous learning, career advancement, and the chance to work on challenging, cutting-edge projects.

Building a strong employer brand synonymous with innovation and forward-thinking is key to attracting talent who seek such environments. This reputation extends beyond products or services, encompassing the company's approach to employee development and fostering an innovative mindset.

Additionally, visionary leaders engage with talent communities, be it at industry conferences, online forums, or educational institutions. This engagement allows them to connect with individuals who already display the entrepreneurial characteristics crucial for driving innovation and growth within the company.

FOSTERING INTERDISCIPLINARY COLLABORATION

In the realm of innovation, the merging of diverse disciplines often sparks the most groundbreaking ideas. Visionary leaders understand this and actively work to foster interdisciplinary collaboration within their organizations. This part of the chapter explores the strategies they use to break down silos and encourage effective teamwork among diverse groups.

Visionary leaders often create cross-functional teams,

bringing together members from various departments or expertise areas. These teams offer a blend of perspectives and skills, enriching the environment for innovation. They also cultivate a culture of shared learning, where knowledge exchange across different fields is standard practice. This might include interdisciplinary workshops, joint projects, or team-building activities focused on mutual learning.

The design of collaborative workspaces is also crucial. Visionaries arrange physical spaces to promote interaction, like open-plan offices and communal areas, facilitating easy collaboration among diverse team members. In our digital age, they utilize technology to connect teams, especially those geographically dispersed, investing in tools that enable seamless communication and collaboration.

Setting common goals and objectives is essential to unify diverse teams. Visionaries ensure that, despite varied backgrounds, all members are aligned and working toward shared purposes. They also encourage a holistic understanding of the business, providing training or departmental rotations to foster empathy and collaboration.

Incentivizing collaborative success is another strategy. Leaders implement systems that reward teamwork and joint achievements, motivating teams to work together effectively. Leadership that actively models collaboration sets the tone for the organization, demonstrating the value of working together across different departments.

Fostering an environment of respect and openness is vital for successful collaboration. Visionaries create cultures where all ideas are valued and open expression of differing opinions is safe. Recognizing the need for evolving collaboration strategies, they regularly review and adjust their approaches, staying responsive to feedback and outcomes. This dynamic approach ensures that collaborative efforts remain effective and aligned with the organization's evolving needs and goals.

BREAKING DOWN SILOS

Visionary leaders recognize that silos, be they organizational, departmental, or disciplinary, can hinder innovation. To address this, they implement strategies that facilitate the breakdown of these barriers. One effective approach is encouraging regular interdepartmental communication. By organizing frequent meetings and fostering open channels of communication, they ensure a seamless flow of information across various segments of the organization.

They also initiate shared projects and goals that necessitate collaboration from multiple departments. Such projects compel teams from different areas to work jointly toward a unified objective, thus naturally breaking down siloed mentalities.

Furthermore, these leaders adapt their leadership

structures to be more flexible and less hierarchical. This adaptation fosters a culture where open communication and cooperation are not just possible but actively encouraged across different business areas. This kind of leadership structure is integral in promoting a collaborative environment, essential for driving innovation and holistic growth within the organization.

ENCOURAGING EXPERIMENTATION IN THE WORKPLACE

Futuristic strategists recognize that at the heart of innovation lies the willingness to experiment. Experimentation fosters a culture of inquiry, exploration, and, ultimately, breakthroughs in creativity and problem-solving. This section of the chapter will focus on how leaders can create an environment conducive to experimentation and productive creativity.

CREATING A SAFE SPACE FOR EXPERIMENTATION

Leaders focused on innovation foster a culture where failure is seen as an integral part of the learning journey. They communicate to their teams that it's safe to take calculated risks and view setbacks as opportunities for growth and improvement. Simultaneously, while encouraging creativity, they set clear boundaries and guidelines to ensure that all experimentation aligns with the organization's goals and values.

Access to necessary resources is crucial for effective

experimentation. Visionary leaders ensure their teams have what they need, be it time, budget, or specific tools and technologies. They also encourage diverse thinking and approaches to problem-solving, prompting teams to look at challenges from various angles and consider unconventional solutions.

Regular brainstorming sessions play a vital role in this environment. These sessions provide a platform for free-flowing ideas and collaborative thinking, often leading to innovative solutions. Finally, recognizing and rewarding efforts toward experimentation and innovation significantly motivates teams. This recognition can take many forms, from formal programs and bonuses to public acknowledgment of the efforts made, all contributing to a vibrant, innovative organizational culture.

BALANCING AUTONOMY AND ACCOUNTABILITY

While promoting a culture of experimentation, visionary leaders also understand the importance of balancing autonomy with accountability. Here's how they strike this balance.

Leaders aiming to drive innovation grant their teams the autonomy to explore and experiment while simultaneously setting clear expectations and objectives. This approach ensures teams have the freedom to innovate yet remain aligned with the organization's overall goals. Regular check-ins and constructive feedback are essential in maintaining a balance between independence and oversight. These interactions provide opportunities to discuss progress, tackle challenges, and realign efforts as needed.

These leaders also empower their teams to make decisions within specific boundaries, fostering a sense of ownership and responsibility. At the same time, they ensure actions align with the company's strategic direction. Tracking the progress of experimental projects is facilitated by implementing metrics and setting milestones. This strategy allows leaders to oversee developments without micromanaging, striking a balance between autonomy and accountability.

Creating a transparent reporting structure is critical. While teams are free to experiment, a clear line of visibility is maintained for leaders to monitor progress and step in when necessary. Furthermore, post-experiment reviews and reflective learning sessions are encouraged. These reviews help teams to understand what was successful, identify areas for improvement, and refine processes, which is vital for ensuring accountability and fostering continuous improvement.

SOLICITING DIVERSE IDEAS AND PERSPECTIVES

In an ever-evolving business landscape, the infusion of diverse ideas and perspectives is not just beneficial; it's essential for innovation. Visionary leaders actively seek out and value this diversity in thought. This section of the chapter will focus on the tips for soliciting these diverse viewpoints and how leaders ensure they are incorporated effectively within an organization.

ACTIVELY SEEKING DIVERSE IDEAS

Creating an environment where every team member feels valued and empowered to contribute is a cornerstone of visionary leadership. These leaders cultivate an inclusive culture where a range of viewpoints is not only tolerated but actively sought out and celebrated. As part of this effort, they focus on assembling teams with diverse backgrounds, experiences, and skill sets, recognizing that such diversity is a key driver of innovative solutions. This commitment to diversity extends to hiring practices and team formation.

To further encourage the flow of diverse perspectives, visionary leaders implement open forums, suggestion boxes, or digital platforms where employees can freely share their ideas. These platforms are particularly effective in empowering those who might be less comfortable voicing their opinions in traditional meetings. Leaders also encourage contrarian thinking, urging team members to question existing ideas and propose alternative viewpoints, a practice that often leads to deeper analysis and more innovative solutions.

Additionally, regular diversity training and awareness programs are conducted to sensitize team members to the importance of varied perspectives. These programs typically cover topics such as unconscious bias, cultural competence, and effective communication across diverse groups, helping to build a more understanding and collaborative workforce.

CULTIVATING CONTINUOUS LEARNING AND DEVELOPMENT

Trailblazing innovators understand that an organization's ability to innovate is closely tied to its commitment to continuous learning and development. Here's how they cultivate this culture:

Offering personalized learning opportunities tailored to each employee's career aspirations and skill gaps is a key strategy for fostering professional growth. This could range from providing access to online courses and workshops to organizing seminars. Additionally, implementing mentorship and coaching programs allows employees to gain insights and guidance from more experienced colleagues or external experts, aiding both personal and professional development.

Visionary leaders also encourage cross-functional experiences, allowing employees to work on projects outside their usual scope or in different departments. This approach broadens their understanding of the business and sparks new ideas. Investing in professional development is also crucial, with leaders allocating budgets for employees to attend conferences, industry events, or pursue further education, showing a commitment to their team's growth.

Creating a culture that values learning from both success and failure is essential. Leaders encourage teams to debrief and share lessons from all experiences, ensuring continuous improvement and development. Regular feedback and performance reviews are also integral, focusing not just on results but also on learning and development goals, helping employees to continually advance in their roles and careers.

By implementing these strategies, visionary leaders ensure that a wide range of voices is heard and valued within their organization. They create an environment where diverse ideas are the fuel for innovation and where continuous learning and personal development are integral to the organizational culture. This approach not only drives creativity and innovation but also contributes to employee satisfaction and retention.

ENCOURAGING RISK-TAKING AND EMBRACING FAILURE

For a culture of innovation to truly flourish, an organization must embrace risk-taking and normalize failure as a part of the learning process. Forward-thinking pioneers are adept at fostering this mindset, understanding that the path to groundbreaking innovation often involves navigating uncertainties and learning from missteps.

This section of the chapter explores the measures leaders put in place to support a culture where taking risks and learning from failures are integral aspects of the organizational ethos.

CREATING A SAFE ENVIRONMENT FOR RISK-TAKING

Futuristic strategists focus on redefining failure within the organizational context, viewing it not as a setback but as a crucial source of insight and learning. They emphasize that each failure is a stepping stone toward innovation and encourage their teams to adopt this perspective. Alongside this, they set clear expectations around risk-taking, ensuring that it aligns with the organization's goals and values. There's a distinct understanding of what constitutes a calculated, worthwhile risk versus reckless, unwarranted risks.

Creating an environment where employees feel psychologically safe to take risks is also essential. This is achieved by fostering a culture of trust, empathy, and open communication, where team members feel supported and understood. Additionally, leaders encourage small-scale experimentation, promoting the use of pilot projects or limited-scope trials as a means to test new ideas with minimized risk. This approach allows for a process of learning and iterating that is less daunting and more manageable without the pressure of extensive consequences. Through these practices, visionary leaders cultivate a workplace that values innovation and smart risk-taking.

LEARNING AND GROWING FROM FAILURE

After a project or experiment doesn't go as planned, visionary leaders take the time to conduct debriefing sessions. These sessions are crucial for dissecting what occurred, understanding the lessons learned, and determining how these insights can be applied in the future. In some organizations, practices like 'failure forums' have been established, where teams openly share their unsuccessful experiences and the knowledge gained from them. This approach helps in destigmatizing failure and, instead, celebrates the learning that emerges from these experiences.

Another important strategy is the adjustment of performance metrics to include innovation efforts, even when they don't always lead to immediate success. By doing so, leaders foster a culture that encourages risk-taking. Performance evaluations in such environments recognize efforts toward innovation and creativity, not just the final outcomes.

Providing adequate support and resources to teams, particularly following a setback, is also vital. This support could manifest in various forms, such as additional training, mentoring, or simply ensuring that teams have the necessary tools and resources to recover, learn, and embark on new initiatives. Through these approaches, visionary leaders build a resilient and innovative organizational culture that values learning and continuous improvement.

BALANCING RISK WITH PRUDENCE

While encouraging risk-taking, visionary leaders also ensure a balance between risk and prudent strategy.

Visionary leaders employ risk assessment frameworks to evaluate the potential impact of new ideas or projects. This careful evaluation aids in making informed decisions about which risks are prudent to pursue. They also promote a balanced approach to innovation projects, akin to managing a diverse investment portfolio. Not all projects carry high risks; some are designed for stable, incremental innovations, which offset the uncertainty of more radical, high-risk endeavors.

Continuous monitoring and the ability to pivot or adjust strategies based on new information or market changes are also integral to this approach. Visionary leaders keep a close watch on ongoing projects, ensuring they can adapt quickly to new developments or insights.

At the core of their leadership philosophy is the belief that risk-taking is a vital component of innovation. They foster a culture where failure isn't dreaded but embraced as an invaluable source of growth and learning. By implementing these strategies, they create an environment that celebrates the risk and discovery inherent in the pursuit of innovation, cultivating a forward-thinking and resilient organizational culture.

INNOVATIVE REWARD AND RECOGNITION SYSTEMS

In a culture that values innovation, the ways in which contributions and breakthroughs are acknowledged and celebrated can significantly impact the motivation and engagement of the team. Visionary leaders understand that traditional reward systems may not fully capture the essence of creative contributions.

Therefore, they often implement innovative reward and recognition systems designed to specifically acknowledge and incentivize innovation. This section of the chapter explores the types of systems that are effective in such a culture.

TYPES OF REWARD AND RECOGNITION SYSTEMS IN A CULTURE OF INNOVATION

Visionary leaders emphasize the importance of innovation in performance metrics, incorporating indicators like the number of new ideas generated, the implementation of innovative solutions, or contributions to patent filings. This shift acknowledges innovation as a crucial component of performance evaluation.

To further encourage innovation, they implement spot awards or immediate recognition for team members who propose novel ideas or solutions. These awards can range from monetary bonuses and gift cards to public acknowledgment in team meetings. Additionally, organizing regular innovation challenges or competitions can stimulate creativity. Winners might receive unique rewards such as the chance to work on special projects, professional development grants, or company-wide recognition.

Publicly acknowledging employees' innovative achievements in company communications, such as newsletters or team meetings, also plays a vital role in boosting morale and inspiring others to contribute their ideas. Offering employees time to work on personal projects is another powerful incentive. This approach, famously used by Google with their '20% time' policy, allows employees to spend a portion of their work time on personal projects or exploring new ideas.

Providing clear pathways for career advancement linked to innovative contributions is also key. This could mean promotions, leadership roles, or spearheading new initiatives. For particularly promising ideas, visionary leaders offer resources and support to further develop these ideas, potentially providing funding, a dedicated team, or mentorship.

Lastly, understanding individual motivators and offering customized rewards is crucial. While some may be motivated by public recognition, others might value additional learning opportunities or financial incentives. This tailored approach ensures that rewards resonate with each individual's unique preferences and motivations.

CELEBRATING CREATIVE CONTRIBUTIONS AND BREAKTHROUGHS

Visionary leaders complement their reward systems by cultivating a culture that regularly celebrates innovation in various ways. They host regular events where teams can showcase their innovative projects or ideas, providing a platform for recognition and inspiring others within the organization. Success stories of innovations and the teams behind them are shared in company meetings or through internal communication channels, highlighting the value placed on innovation.

To further honor groundbreaking work, some leaders establish a 'hall of fame' for significant innovations and the employees responsible for them. This can be a dedicated space in the office or a feature on the company's intranet. Importantly, they acknowledge the efforts and processes involved in innovation, not just the successful outcomes. Recognizing the hard work and experimentation that goes into innovation encourages continued risk-taking and creative thinking.

By implementing these varied approaches to reward and recognition, visionary leaders ensure that creativity and innovation are tangibly valued and celebrated within their organizations. This strategy not only motivates employees to think creatively but also cultivates a strong, pervasive culture of innovation throughout the company.

CHAPTER 5
MAKING BOLD MOVES EARLY

IN THE REALM of visionary leadership, the ability to make early, decisive moves often sets apart the trailblazers from the followers. At the heart of these pivotal decisions lies a crucial, yet often underestimated, tool—instinct. This chapter delves into the role that intuition plays in the decision-making process of visionary leaders, especially in scenarios where empirical data is limited or non-existent.

THE POWER OF INSTINCT IN LEADERSHIP

Visionary leaders frequently encounter situations where the data at hand is either insufficient or too ambiguous to inform a clear-cut decision. In such scenarios, instinct—an inner compass shaped by experience, knowledge, and foresight—takes the helm. This instinct is not a wild guess but an informed intuition that has been honed over years of experience, successes, and failures.

INTUITION AND EARLY DECISION-MAKING

Visionary leaders often excel in their ability to recognize patterns and trends that aren't immediately obvious to others. They harness their instincts, honed through past experiences, to connect the dots and make educated assumptions about the future. Their experience, encompassing both successes and failures, plays a significant role in shaping these instincts, contributing to an intuitive understanding of what might work in any given situation.

These leaders often rely on their intuition, especially in situations marked by uncertainty. In such scenarios, waiting for perfect data can mean missing out on crucial opportunities. Visionary leaders understand that making timely decisions, guided by intuition, can often be a decisive factor in success. A real-world example of this is Steve Jobs' decision to develop the iPhone. Despite the lack of concrete data predicting its success, Jobs relied on his instincts about consumer behavior and technology trends, a decision that revolutionized the smartphone industry.

Instinct-based decision-making also involves a careful balance between risk and opportunity. Trailblazing innovators are skilled at quickly assessing the potential upsides and downsides of decisions when conclusive data is unavailable. They have an innate ability to weigh the risks against the potential rewards, allowing them to make bold moves that others might shy away from, often leading to groundbreaking innovations and industry leadership.

CULTIVATING AND TRUSTING YOUR INSTINCT

But how do these leaders develop and come to trust their instincts to such an extent? This chapter explores various ways through which intuition can be cultivated and refined.

Visionary leaders maintain a commitment to continuous learning, ensuring they stay updated with industry trends and developments. This ongoing education builds a reservoir of knowledge that significantly informs their instincts. Additionally, they engage in reflective practices, analyzing their past decision-making patterns, successes, and failures. This reflection helps in finetuning their intuitive skills, making them more reliable and accurate over time.

Another key practice among visionary leaders is seeking diverse perspectives. By consulting a broad range of viewpoints, they ensure that their intuition is informed by a well-rounded understanding of different situations and scenarios. This exposure to varied perspectives contributes to the development of wellinformed instincts.

Furthermore, these leaders don't just rely on their intuition blindly. They test and validate their gut feelings through smaller, less risky decisions. This approach allows them to gradually build confidence in their intuitive judgments, helping them to rely on their instincts more confidently when making significant decisions. This process of continuous learning, reflection, seeking diverse inputs, and testing their instincts enables visionary leaders to make more informed and effective decisions, even in the absence of complete data.

CAPITALIZING ON FIRST-MOVER ADVANTAGE

Gaining the first-mover advantage in any industry can be a game-changing strategy for visionary leaders. Visionaries identify and capitalize on opportunities to advance significantly before their competitors, positioning their companies not just to participate in the market but to lead it.

STRATEGIES FOR SEIZING FIRST-MOVER ADVANTAGE

Visionary leaders adeptly combine foresight, strategic planning, and swift execution to secure a first-mover advantage in their markets. Their success begins with an acute ability to identify and analyze emerging trends. By keeping a close watch on market shifts, technological advancements, and changes in consumer behavior, they are often the first to spot new opportunities.

Once they identify a potential opportunity, they move quickly to prototype and test their ideas in the market. This rapid iteration process is crucial for refining their offerings and getting ahead of competitors. Strategic resource allocation is another key aspect of their approach. Visionaries prioritize funding, talent, and other essential resources, ensuring swift development and launch of new products or services.

Building a flexible and agile team is also a part of their strategy. These leaders cultivate a workforce capable of quickly adapting to new directives and efficiently working toward market introduction of new concepts. Given that first movers often encounter uncharted territory, effective risk management becomes essential. Visionary leaders are skilled in identifying and mitigating potential risks associated with pioneering a new market segment.

A strong value proposition is crucial for cementing a first-mover advantage. These leaders focus on creating offerings that are not only the first to market but also distinctly superior to anything currently available or likely to follow. In industries where innovations are easily replicated, securing intellectual property rights is critical. By protecting their innovations legally, visionaries maintain a competitive edge over those who enter the market later.

Lastly, visionary leaders recognize the power of strategic partnerships and alliances. By identifying potential partners who can expedite their go-to-market strategy or provide essential components or technology, they can move even faster. A notable example of this approach is Netflix's early transition from DVD rentals to streaming. Recognizing the potential of streaming technology, Netflix swiftly shifted its business model, outpacing traditional media companies and establishing itself as a leader in the emerging online streaming industry. This move was bolstered by strategic partnerships with content creators and distributors, solidifying Netflix's position as a trailblazer in the media and entertainment sector.

IDENTIFYING OPPORTUNITIES FOR FIRST-MOVER ADVANTAGE

Visionary leaders employ a range of strategies to identify the right opportunities for gaining a first-mover advantage. One key approach is engaging in continuous market research. By keeping a constant pulse on the market through research and customer feedback, they can pinpoint gaps and emerging opportunities. They also leverage data analytics tools extensively, analyzing large sets of data to uncover insights into evolving trends and potential market openings.

Additionally, these leaders recognize the value of cultivating a diverse network. By connecting with industry experts, customers, and other stakeholders, they gain a broader perspective and early signals of potential opportunities. This network acts as a vital source of information, offering various viewpoints and insights that might not be apparent from data alone.

Encouraging a culture of innovation within their organizations is also crucial. They promote an environment where every team member is encouraged to think innovatively and propose new ideas. This approach fosters a continuous stream of fresh perspectives and creative solutions, increasing the likelihood of discovering unique first-mover opportunities. By integrating these methods, visionary leaders adeptly position their organizations to identify and capitalize on opportunities that set them apart in the market.

BALANCING INSTINCT AND DATA

The art of balancing instinct with data analysis is a critical skill for visionary leaders, especially in an age where decisions can have far-reaching consequences. This section of Chapter 5 explores the frameworks and methodologies visionary leaders use to strike a balance between gut feelings and empirical evidence in their decision-making processes.

FRAMEWORKS FOR BALANCING INSTINCT AND DATA

Visionary leaders skillfully blend data with their instincts to make informed decisions. They start by gathering as much relevant data as possible and then overlay this information with their instincts, which are sharpened by experience and knowledge. This method enables them to make decisions that are not only data-driven but also intuitively sound.

In situations where data is incomplete or inconclusive, these leaders often resort to scenario planning. They create a range of potential scenarios based on available data and use their instincts to assess the likelihood and impact of these scenarios. Over time, these futuristic strategists develop a nuanced intuition for interpreting data and understanding its context, underlying trends, and potential biases, which go beyond mere numerical analysis.

Implementing a feedback loop system is another strategy they use. Initial decisions are made using a mix of data and instinct, followed by a phase of careful monitoring and evaluation. This process allows for adjustments based on new data or analyzed outcomes, ensuring a balanced approach between data and intuition.

Moreover, visionary leaders often employ a risk assessment matrix to guide their decision-making process. This matrix helps in evaluating the potential risks of a decision against the likelihood of various outcomes, effectively quantifying the process and aiding in determining when to rely on gut feelings and when to wait for more data.

A real-world example of this approach can be seen in Netflix's decision to shift from DVD rentals to streaming. Netflix's leadership, led by Reed Hastings, used data to understand shifting consumer preferences and technological trends. However, the move into streaming was also a bold leap based on instinct about the future of entertainment consumption. The feedback loop system of continuously analyzing viewership data and adjusting content offerings has since become a hallmark of Netflix's strategy, demonstrating a harmonious blend of data and instinct in decision-making.

DETERMINING WHEN TO TRUST INSTINCT VS. DATA

Visionary leaders adeptly navigate the balance between relying on instinct and seeking additional data by considering various factors. In situations where quick decision-making is essential, they might lean more heavily on their instincts, particularly if waiting for more data could result in missed opportunities. The availability and quality of the existing data are crucial considerations. In cases where data is scarce or unreliable, they may depend more on their experience and intuition.

The nature of the decision also plays a significant role in this balance. For strategic, long-term decisions, leaders often prefer data-driven approaches. However, for decisions requiring quick responses or those based on ever-changing market dynamics, instinct might be more heavily weighted.

Reflecting on past experiences and outcomes is another critical aspect. Leaders consider previous instances where they relied on their instincts and the results of those decisions. This reflection helps inform the extent to which they should trust their gut feelings in current situations.

Moreover, consulting with trusted advisors or colleagues offers a broader perspective and challenges their thinking, helping to strike a balance between instinct and data. By weighing these factors, visionary leaders make informed decisions that blend the best of both instinctive and data-driven approaches.

AGILITY IN DECISION-MAKING

In today's fast-paced and ever-changing business environment, agility in decision-making is not just an advantage; it's a necessity for visionary leaders. This agility allows leaders to respond swiftly to market changes, technological advancements, and emerging opportunities. This part of Chapter 5 discusses the importance of this agility and how visionary leaders maintain the flexibility to make quick decisions and, when necessary, course-correct.

THE IMPORTANCE OF AGILE DECISION-MAKING

Agile decision-making is crucial in today's fast-paced business environment for several key reasons. Firstly, it enables organizations to rapidly respond to changes in market dynamics. In a landscape where conditions can shift overnight, the ability to make quick decisions helps organizations stay ahead of competitors by responding promptly to these changes.

Secondly, agility in decision-making allows leaders to capitalize on emerging opportunities that might be fleeting. By making swift decisions, they can seize these opportunities before they disappear, giving their organizations a competitive edge.

Lastly, quick decision-making is also vital in mitigating risks. It enables leaders to either avoid potential pitfalls or minimize their impact, thereby safeguarding the organization from possible adverse outcomes. This aspect of agility in decision-making is crucial in navigating the uncertain waters of the business world effectively.

STRATEGIES FOR MAINTAINING DECISION-MAKING AGILITY

Forward-thinking pioneers in the business world adopt a range of strategies to enhance agility in their decision-making. They empower their teams by delegating decision-making authority, especially to those individuals or groups closer to the core operations. This delegation, supported by clear guidelines, cultivates quicker decision-making, with leaders placing trust in their teams to make informed choices within set parameters.

Streamlining processes is another crucial strategy. By simplifying and reducing bureaucracy in decision-making processes, leaders ensure that delays are minimized. This could mean having fewer layers of approval or adopting more flexible policies. Alongside this, they foster a culture of trust and accountability, where employees feel empowered to make decisions and are responsible for the outcomes, further accelerating the decision-making process.

The use of technology, such as data analytics tools and AI, also plays a significant role. These tools provide real-time insights and predictions, aiding in faster and more accurate decision-making. Regular review sessions and feedback loops are implemented to quickly assess the impact of decisions and make necessary adjustments, ensuring that the organization remains dynamic and responsive.

Scenario planning and having contingency measures in place are also part of their approach. By preparing for various scenarios, leaders can make quicker decisions, comforted by the knowledge that fallback options are available if needed. Additionally, instilling a mindset of flexibility and adaptability among team members is key. This mindset prepares them to anticipate changes and react positively to shifts in plans or strategies.

An illustrative example of this approach can be seen in Amazon's expansion into cloud computing with Amazon Web Services (AWS). Amazon empowered its teams to explore and develop cloud computing solutions, streamlining processes to encourage innovation. The company's culture of trust and its use of advanced technology allowed it to quickly adapt to the emerging cloud computing market. Regular reviews and a clear contingency plan further enabled Amazon to make swift decisions in developing AWS, which has since become a major part of its business model. This agility in decision-making and the willingness to adapt and innovate have been crucial in Amazon's growth and continued success.

COURSE-CORRECTING WHEN NECESSARY

Visionary leaders understand that the ability to course-correct is as crucial as making quick decisions. They diligently monitor the outcomes of their decisions, which enables them to quickly identify when adjustments are necessary. Actively seeking and embracing feedback is another key aspect of their approach. They solicit input from teams, customers, and other stakeholders, gaining insights that may necessitate a change in direction.

Maintaining open lines of communication within the organization is also vital. This open communication ensures that information is shared freely and swiftly, facilitating timely course corrections when needed. Additionally, visionary leaders view each decision as an opportunity to learn and grow. They are quick to adapt their strategies based on the lessons learned from both their successes and failures, continually refining their approach in response to new information and changing circumstances.

This combination of continuous monitoring, embracing feedback, open communication, and a willingness to learn and adapt enables visionary leaders to navigate complex and dynamic environments effectively.

PREDICTING AND BETTING ON FUTURE TRENDS

Visionary leaders have a remarkable ability to not only predict future trends but also to place strategic bets on them. Their success often hinges on their foresight and understanding of which trends will significantly impact their industry.

Chapter 5 delves into the methods these leaders use to identify these trends and the strategies they employ to manage the risks associated with early decision-making based on often limited information.

IDENTIFYING FUTURE TRENDS

Visionary leaders employ a multifaceted approach to identify future trends that might impact their industry. A significant part of this process is leveraging data analytics to gather insights into emerging trends. This involves analyzing various factors such as consumer behavior, market shifts, and technological advancements to spot patterns that could signal future developments.

Networking with thought leaders, attending industry conferences, and staying engaged with innovation hubs also play a crucial role. These interactions keep visionaries informed about potential future trends and provide valuable insights. In addition, regular market research, including surveys and focus groups, is conducted to understand consumer needs and preferences, often serving as early indicators of new trends.

Scenario analysis is another method employed by these leaders. They explore how different future trends might unfold and assess their potential impact on the industry. This technique aids in understanding the implications of each emerging trend. Moreover, visionary leaders closely monitor global events and socio-economic changes. Shifts in global dynamics, economic fluctuations, and changes in consumer lifestyles can all herald significant industry trends, making it crucial for leaders to be aware of these broader factors. Through this comprehensive approach, visionary leaders effectively anticipate and prepare for changes that could shape the future of their industry.

MANAGING RISKS IN EARLY DECISION-MAKING

When navigating decisions based on predictions of future trends, visionary leaders are keenly aware of the need to manage associated risks, particularly when information is limited. A key strategy they employ is the diversification of bets. Rather than investing all their resources in one specific trend or innovation, they spread their investments across multiple potential trends. This approach mitigates risk and increases the likelihood of identifying a successful trend.

Before fully committing to a trend, these leaders often initiate pilot projects or develop prototypes. These smaller-scale tests allow them to gather more information and validate the trend with a lower level of risk involved. Once a decision to pursue a particular trend is made, continuous monitoring is essential. This ongoing vigilance allows for quick adjustments if needed. Leaders maintain flexibility to pivot their strategies based on new information or if the trend doesn't evolve as initially anticipated.

The agility and resilience of their teams are also crucial in this process. By preparing their teams to be adaptable, leaders ensure that the organization can swiftly respond to changes and unexpected outcomes from early trend-based decisions.

Moreover, visionary leaders utilize structured risk assessment frameworks to carefully evaluate the potential impact of following a trend. This evaluation includes analyzing worst-case scenarios, assessing the likelihood of various outcomes, and considering the organization's capacity to respond effectively. Through these combined efforts, visionary leaders effectively balance the pursuit of emerging trends with the prudent management of associated risks.

FOSTERING A PROACTIVE ORGANIZATIONAL CULTURE

=For a company to consistently stay ahead of the curve, fostering a proactive organizational culture is essential. Visionary leaders understand this and implement specific practices to encourage their employees to take initiative and make bold moves.

ENCOURAGING PROACTIVE AND EARLY DECISION-MAKING

Visionary leaders implement a range of organizational practices to encourage a proactive approach within their teams. Central to this is empowering employees. By granting employees the authority and autonomy to make decisions, leaders encourage them to take ownership of their projects and ideas, fostering a sense of responsibility and initiative.

Creating a supportive environment is also essential. In this environment, risk-taking is encouraged and not penalized, ensuring that employees feel safe to explore new ideas and approaches. The knowledge that they won't face negative repercussions for ideas that don't pan out as expected is key to promoting innovation.

Setting clear goals and expectations is another important aspect. While fostering initiative, it's crucial for leaders to provide clear guidance to ensure that employees' efforts align with the organization's objectives. This clarity helps in channeling their energy and creativity in the right direction.

Leaders also focus on promoting a forward-thinking mindset among their teams. Through training and development programs, employees are encouraged to constantly look for better and more efficient ways of doing things. This mindset keeps the team-oriented toward continuous improvement and innovation.

Rewarding initiative plays a significant role as well. When leaders recognize and reward employees who show initiative and are willing to make bold moves, it not only reinforces the value placed on these behaviors but also motivates others to exhibit similar proactivity.

Encouraging cross-departmental collaboration is

another strategy employed by visionary leaders. Such collaboration creates opportunities for employees to gain new perspectives and insights. This, in turn, can spark proactive problem-solving and innovation, as employees are exposed to diverse ideas and ways of thinking. By integrating these practices, visionary leaders create a dynamic and proactive organizational culture.

LEARNING FROM EARLY FAILURES OR MISSTEPS

Visionary leaders not only foster early and bold decision-making but also cultivate a learning environment where early failures are viewed as valuable learning experiences. One of their key approaches is normalizing failure. They treat it as an essential part of the learning and innovation process, emphasizing to their teams that failures are not setbacks but stepping stones to future success.

After any failure, they conduct thorough post-mortem analyses to understand what went wrong and why. Involving their teams in these discussions is crucial for extracting valuable learning points from the experience. These insights are then used to adapt and refine their strategies. Visionary leaders demonstrate an ability to pivot based on new learnings, underscoring that adaptability is just as important as persistence.

Moreover, they share the lessons learned from failures throughout the organization, transforming individual missteps into collective learning opportunities.

This approach ensures that the entire organization benefits from the insights gained from any failed endeavor.

Fostering a growth mindset among employees is another focus. Leaders encourage their teams to view challenges and failures as opportunities for growth and improvement. They also promote reflective practices, urging regular reflection on both successes and failures. This reflection helps teams understand their decision-making processes and identify areas for improvement, fostering a culture of continuous learning and development.

CHAPTER 6
CREATING ORGANIZATIONAL AGILITY

IN AN ERA MARKED by rapid technological advancements and constantly evolving market dynamics, the structure of an organization plays a pivotal role in its success and longevity. Visionary leaders, aware of these changing tides, design their organizations for maximum flexibility and agility, drawing a stark contrast to traditional, rigid hierarchical models.

This approach is evident in companies like Google, which adopts a flexible organizational structure, encouraging open communication and cross-functional collaboration, enabling it to remain at the forefront of technological innovation. Similarly, Spotify's use of autonomous "squads" that operate like mini-startups within the company showcases how agility can be ingrained in an organization's structure.

These squads are empowered to make decisions quickly and independently, allowing Spotify to innovate and respond to market changes rapidly. In contrast, more traditional organizations with rigid hierarchies, like many legacy corporations, often find themselves struggling to keep pace with such nimble competitors. They tend to face challenges in responding swiftly to market shifts, as decision-making in these structures can be slowed down by multiple layers of bureaucracy.

Visionary leaders understand that in today's dynamic business environment, an organization's ability to adapt quickly to new technologies and market changes is not just an advantage but a necessity. By structuring their organizations for flexibility and agility, they foster environments that are primed for innovation, quick decision-making, and rapid adaptation to change.

THE SHIFT FROM RIGIDITY TO FLEXIBILITY

The conventional hierarchical structure, characterized by its rigid layers and top-down decision-making processes, has long been the standard in the business world. However, visionary leaders recognize that such rigidity can stifle innovation and slow down the organization's ability to respond to change. Instead, they advocate for and implement more flexible, flat structures.

CHARACTERISTICS OF FLEXIBLE ORGANIZATIONAL STRUCTURES

The implementation of flat and decentralized hierarchies is a key factor in elevating your leadership. These flattened structures eliminate unnecessary layers, promoting closer communication and swifter decision-making. In these organizations, the focus shifts to decentralization, with decision-making authority spread throughout the organization, encouraging more people to participate in key decisions.

Employees in such organizations often work in cross-functional teams. These teams, composed of members with diverse skill sets and perspectives, foster collaboration and innovation. This approach allows teams to have a more holistic view of projects, moving away from the limitations of working in silos. It empowers teams to be more effective and creative in tackling various challenges.

Open and transparent communication is another cornerstone of these flexible structures. Leaders in these organizations encourage environments where information flows freely. This open communication ensures that all team members, regardless of their position in the hierarchy, have access to the necessary information, fostering inclusivity and collaboration.

Leadership within these flexible structures tends to be more adaptive. Leaders function more as facilitators and coaches rather than as traditional authoritative figures. This adaptive leadership style allows for greater autonomy and engagement among employees. It encourages initiative and innovation, with leaders guiding teams rather than micromanaging them.

A real-world example of this approach is Spotify's

use of autonomous "squads." Spotify's structure consists of small, cross-functional teams (squads), each operating like a mini-startup. These squads have the autonomy to decide what they work on and how they work, promoting agility and innovation. This structure facilitates rapid decision-making and adaptability, key to Spotify's success in the dynamic and competitive world of music streaming. The company's organizational model illustrates how visionary leadership and flexible structures can drive innovation and adaptability in a fast-paced industry.

IMPACT ON ADAPTABILITY AND INNOVATION

The move towards more flexible organizational structures significantly enhances an organization's adaptability and capacity for innovation. One of the primary benefits of flat structures is the ability to respond more quickly to changes in the market or industry. With fewer hierarchical layers, decisions can be made and implemented swiftly, enabling the organization to stay agile in a fast-paced business environment.

Such flexible structures also foster an environment that is highly conducive to innovation. By empowering teams and encouraging open communication, these structures ensure that employees feel more invested in their work. This sense of ownership and inclusion makes employees more likely to contribute innovative and creative ideas, driving the organization forward.

Additionally, flat organizational structures tend to boost employee engagement and satisfaction. In environments where employees feel their voices are heard and their contributions are valued, there is generally a higher level of motivation and commitment. This increased engagement not only benefits the employees but also enhances the overall productivity and effectiveness of the organization.

However, adopting flexible structures is not without its challenges. Maintaining alignment across the organization and ensuring effective coordination can be complex. Trailblazing innovators must skillfully balance the need for some level of structure with the desire for flexibility. This balancing act is crucial for reaping the benefits of a flat and decentralized organization while mitigating potential drawbacks such as misalignment or coordination difficulties.

BUILDING AND EMPOWERING NIMBLE TEAMS

Visionary leaders adopt strategic approaches to create and manage nimble teams, focusing on diversity in skills, backgrounds, and thought processes. They prioritize selecting individuals who are not just skilled but also adaptable, collaborative, and open to new learning opportunities. This selective recruitment ensures that the team composition aligns with the organization's dynamic needs.

A key emphasis is placed on fostering a collaborative

culture. In contrast to environments that prioritize individual brilliance, leaders in these organizations encourage team members to work closely together, sharing ideas freely and leveraging each other's strengths for collective success. This collaborative approach is essential for the high-functioning of nimble teams.

Encouraging autonomy and ownership is another critical aspect. Members of nimble teams are given a significant degree of autonomy and are motivated to take full ownership of their projects. This empowerment enables them to make decisions, solve problems, and innovate without needing constant oversight.

Cross-functional integration is a hallmark of nimble teams. These teams often include members from various departments, fostering a broader perspective and more holistic problem-solving approach. This integration is crucial for addressing complex challenges that require diverse insights.

Continuous skill development is also a focus. Visionary leaders invest in the ongoing training and development of their teams, ensuring they are equipped with the latest knowledge and tools necessary to adapt to new challenges and stay at the forefront of their fields.

Many nimble teams operate using agile methodologies, which emphasize iterative development, regular feedback, and adaptability to changes. This approach allows teams to respond more swiftly and effectively to challenges and opportunities compared to more traditional, linear methods.

Regular feedback and open communication are essential to keeping these teams aligned with the organization's goals. Engaging in regular feedback sessions helps to quickly address any issues or bottlenecks, ensuring the team remains on track.

Finally, empowering leaders within teams is a unique feature of this approach. Instead of relying solely on a single leader, nimble teams often have multiple members who can assume leadership roles as needed. This flexibility allows for dynamic leadership depending on the specific project or situation, further enhancing the team's agility and responsiveness.

OPERATING DIFFERENTLY FROM INDIVIDUAL-CENTRIC ORGANIZATIONS

Nimble teams present a contrast to traditional organizations that emphasize individual brilliance with distinct operational differences.

In environments where teams have mastered this, problem-solving is a collective effort. Challenges are tackled using the diverse skills and perspectives of the entire team. This approach is distinct from environments where solutions are expected to originate from individual genius. It leverages the collective intelligence of the group, leading to more innovative and comprehensive solutions.

There's a strong sense of shared responsibility and credit in these teams. Successes and failures are not attributed to individuals alone but are seen as collective outcomes. This shared responsibility fosters a sense of teamwork and reduces the pressure on any single member to always be the standout performer.

Members of nimble teams often exhibit dynamic role flexibility. Unlike traditional teams with static role definitions, these team members wear multiple hats, contributing to various aspects of a project as needed. This flexibility allows the team to adapt quickly to new requirements or challenges, ensuring that the right skills are applied to each task.

Nimble teams are particularly responsive and adaptive to change, making them well-suited for fast-paced and unpredictable environments. Their structure and team dynamics are designed to respond quickly to changing circumstances, which is a key advantage in rapidly evolving industries. This responsiveness ensures that nimble teams can pivot as required, maintaining their effectiveness even in the face of unforeseen challenges.

RAPID PROTOTYPING AND ITERATIVE DEVELOPMENT

Rapid prototyping and iterative development are essential elements in fostering organizational agility. These methodologies are not just tools for product development; they are fundamental to an agile organization's

DNA. Visionary leaders integrate these techniques into their standard operating procedures to encourage innovation, adaptability, and responsiveness.

THE ROLE OF RAPID PROTOTYPING

In visionary organizations, rapid prototyping is a key practice that fuels a culture of innovation and agility. Futuristic strategists actively encourage experimentation, allowing teams to quickly and inexpensively test out their ideas. This approach is fundamental to fostering an environment where ideas are not just generated but are also continuously tested and refined.

One of the major advantages of rapid prototyping is the ability to gather feedback early and frequently. By testing prototypes at the earliest stages of development, organizations ensure that their final products are closely aligned with user needs and market demands. This early feedback loop is essential for developing products that truly resonate with users and succeed in the market.

Another significant benefit of rapid prototyping is the reduction in time to market. By accelerating the development process, organizations can launch products faster, giving them a critical edge in competitive industries. This speed to market can be a decisive factor in capturing market share and establishing a product's position in the marketplace.

Moreover, rapid prototyping serves as a vital tool for learning and adaptation. It allows teams to quickly understand what works and what doesn't, facilitating real-time adjustments based on tangible results. This iterative process of learning and adapting helps teams refine their ideas effectively and move toward the most viable and impactful solutions. In essence, rapid prototyping is not just about building products; it's about building knowledge and expertise, making it a cornerstone of innovative organizational practice.

INTEGRATING ITERATIVE DEVELOPMENT

Visionary leaders recognize the value of iterative development, a process that emphasizes gradual improvement through repeated cycles, and integrate it into their operational strategies.

In iterative development, projects are divided into smaller, more manageable cycles. Each cycle involves stages of planning, execution, and evaluation. This breakdown allows for continuous improvement and adjustment at each stage, ensuring that the project evolves effectively in response to new insights and feedback.

A key aspect of iterative development is promoting cross-functional teamwork. Given that these development cycles often require input from various departments, leaders actively foster collaboration across different areas of expertise. This cross-functional collaboration ensures that each iteration benefits from diverse insights and perspectives, enriching the development process.

User-centric design is another priority in iterative development. Each cycle includes user testing and feedback, ensuring that the product or service is continually refined to meet user needs more effectively. This constant focus on the user helps in creating products and services that are truly aligned with what users want and need.

To facilitate iterative development, many organizations adopt Agile methodologies. Methodologies like Scrum or Kanban provide a structured yet flexible framework for organizing work. These frameworks support a responsive approach to project management, allowing teams to adapt quickly to changing requirements and to continuously improve their output. By embracing these methodologies, visionary leaders can guide their teams through the iterative development process, ensuring that their projects remain dynamic and responsive to the fast-paced nature of today's business environment.

INCORPORATING PROTOTYPING AND ITERATION INTO SOPS

Visionary leaders integrate rapid prototyping and iterative development into their organizations by establishing a supportive framework and encouraging a culture that embraces these methodologies:

They start by providing their teams with the necessary training and resources. This ensures that everyone involved has the skills and tools required to engage in rapid prototyping and iterative development effectively. It's about equipping teams with not just the technical know-how but also with the understanding of how these methodologies fit into the larger picture of project development.

Setting clear expectations and metrics is another crucial step. Visionary leaders establish explicit guidelines for using these methodologies and define specific metrics to evaluate their effectiveness. This helps in tracking progress and assessing the impact of these approaches on project outcomes.

Cultivating a responsive mindset among employees is essential. Leaders encourage an organizational culture that values responsiveness, flexibility, and the ability to adapt based on new information or feedback. This mindset shift is critical for the successful implementation of rapid prototyping and iterative development, as it allows teams to pivot quickly and effectively in response to changing circumstances.

Integrating these methodologies with broader organizational goals is also a priority. Visionary leaders ensure that efforts in rapid prototyping and iterative development are aligned with the company's overall strategy. This alignment ensures that these methodologies contribute constructively to the organization's overarching objectives.

Finally, leadership support and involvement are key to embedding these practices into the standard operating procedures. Leaders actively support these methodologies by providing guidance, being involved in the process, and celebrating the successes and learnings that emerge from these approaches. Their involvement not only reinforces the importance of these methodologies but also helps to build a culture where innovation and continuous improvement are valued and practiced consistently.

DATA-DRIVEN DECISION-MAKING IN AGILE ENVIRONMENTS

In an agile organizational structure, the ability to make quick, informed decisions is crucial. Let us now look into how forward-thinking pioneers implement data-driven decision-making within these agile frameworks. We shall examine the balance they strike between the agility required for rapid decision-making and the thoroughness needed for in-depth data analysis.

IMPLEMENTING DATA-DRIVEN DECISION-MAKING IN AGILE SETTINGS

Visionary leaders enhance their organizations' agility by incorporating advanced data practices into their decision-making processes.

One crucial element is integrating real-time data analytics tools. These tools provide quick access to relevant data, enabling faster and more informed decision-making. Leaders ensure that these analytics tools are a core part of the decision-making process, delivering timely insights that guide actions and strategies.

Building data-agile teams is also a priority. Teams are not only trained in understanding data but also in utilizing it effectively. This training includes equipping team members with the skills to analyze and interpret data swiftly. As a result, decisions are made quickly based on a solid understanding of the data at hand.

Streamlining the data collection and analysis processes is another key focus. Visionary leaders work to ensure that these processes are as efficient as possible, preventing them from becoming bottlenecks in the decision-making process. By making data collection and analysis more streamlined, they support rapid decision-making and prevent delays.

Finally, creating a culture of data literacy throughout the organization is essential. In this culture, all employees, regardless of their level or role, are encouraged to incorporate data into their decision-making. This widespread data literacy enhances the overall agility and responsiveness of the organization, as decisions across the board are informed by accurate and timely data insights. This approach not only accelerates the decision-making process but also ensures that these decisions are grounded in real-world data, enhancing their effectiveness and relevance.

BALANCING QUICK DECISION-MAKING WITH THOROUGH DATA ANALYSIS

Visionary leaders adeptly manage the delicate balance between speed and thoroughness in data-driven decision-making by employing several key strategies.

Firstly, they prioritize key data points. Instead of wading through vast amounts of data, leaders focus on the most relevant data points that are critical to the decision at hand. This targeted approach enables quicker yet still effective data analysis, ensuring decisions are based on the most pertinent information.

They also set clear decision-making frameworks. These frameworks provide guidelines on when to opt for quick, data-informed decisions and when more in-depth analysis is warranted. This clarity helps maintain a balance, ensuring that decisions are made swiftly but without compromising on necessary detail and accuracy.

Adopting agile data practices is another crucial element. Practices like iterative data analysis and continuous feedback loops allow organizations to adapt quickly to new information. This agility prevents the need for protracted analysis phases, keeping the decision-making process fluid and responsive.

Decentralizing decision-making also plays a significant role. By empowering individual teams to make informed decisions based on the data available to them, leaders facilitate quicker decision-making processes. This decentralization means decisions don't get bottlenecked waiting for higher-up approvals.

Utilizing predictive analytics is another effective tool. It aids in forecasting trends and potential outcomes, providing foresight that can speed up the decision-making process. Predictive analytics reduce the reliance on extensive historical data analysis, allowing for quicker yet informed decisions.

Finally, visionary leaders regularly review and adjust decision-making processes. This continuous refinement ensures that these processes remain effective and that the right balance between speed and thoroughness is consistently achieved. By doing so, they ensure the decision-making framework evolves in line with the organization's needs and the ever-changing business environment.

BUILDING A DYNAMIC AND FLEXIBLE ORGANIZATIONAL CULTURE

Visionary leaders cultivate a culture that inherently supports continuous learning and swift adaptation, key elements for maintaining organizational agility:

They emphasize the importance of continuous learning and adaptability, providing various opportunities for skill development. This nurturing environment encourages employees to keep up with the latest industry trends and shifts, ensuring that the workforce remains relevant and capable of adapting to new challenges.

Empowering employees is another cornerstone of a dynamic culture. Leaders grant their teams the autonomy to make decisions, fostering a sense of ownership and enabling quick action. This empowerment not only speeds up the decision-making process but also encourages a proactive approach to challenges and opportunities.

Flexible work arrangements are increasingly becoming part of this cultural shift. By allowing options like remote working or flexible hours, leaders demonstrate a commitment to adaptability and personal autonomy. Such policies contribute to a work environment that values flexibility and understands the diverse needs of its workforce.

The adoption of iterative and Agile work processes plays a critical role in ensuring organizational flexibility. These methodologies prioritize regular feedback, adaptability, and continuous improvement. By incorporating these processes, organizations can stay responsive to change, quickly adapting their strategies and operations in the face of new information or shifting market demands. This approach not only keeps the organization nimble but also aligns closely with the evolving expectations of modern employees, who increasingly value dynamic and responsive work environments.

PRACTICES AND CULTURAL NORMS FOR DYNAMISM AND FLEXIBILITY

Visionary leaders employ several key practices to nurture a dynamic and flexible organizational culture:

Promoting open and transparent communication is crucial. Leaders encourage dialogue across all levels of the organization, ensuring a free flow of ideas and feedback. This openness fosters a vibrant, dynamic environment where everyone feels valued and heard.

Recognizing and rewarding flexibility is another important aspect. Leaders actively acknowledge and reward employees who demonstrate adaptability and flexibility, setting a positive example for others to follow.

Encouraging risk-taking and innovation is fundamental to a dynamic culture. Leaders create an environment where creative thinking and experimenting with new ideas are safe and encouraged, establishing norms that favor innovation and out-of-the-box thinking.

Emphasizing diversity and inclusion is also key. A workforce with a range of perspectives and backgrounds is essential for fostering a vibrant culture. Leaders focus on building and nurturing diverse teams and ensuring an inclusive environment where every voice is valued.

Conducting regular organizational assessments and adjustments ensures that the culture remains adaptive and responsive. Leaders are open to reevaluating and adjusting organizational processes and structures to maintain a flexible and dynamic environment.

Leaders themselves model flexibility and adaptability in their actions and decision-making. By embodying these qualities, they set a strong example for the rest of the organization, highlighting the importance of being adaptable in a constantly evolving business landscape.

Finally, celebrating agile successes publicly reinforces the value of flexible and adaptive approaches. Leaders make it a point to publicly acknowledge and celebrate the successes that result from agile methods, encouraging their continued use and emphasizing their importance to the organization's success.

ADAPTING TO MARKET CHANGES AND TECHNOLOGICAL ADVANCEMENTS

Trailblazing innovators have established several vital processes to ensure their organizations remain agile and responsive to change.

A key component is robust environmental scanning. By continuously monitoring the external environment, organizations can promptly identify shifts in market trends, competitor strategies, and technological advancements. This proactive approach involves a keen focus on industry dynamics and emerging technologies.

Flexible strategic planning is essential for agile organizations. Rather than adhering to rigid, long-term plans, these organizations opt for adaptable strategies that can be modified as market conditions and technological landscapes evolve.

Rapid implementation cycles are another hallmark of agile organizations. Instead of lengthy rollouts, changes are implemented in quick cycles, often employing methodologies like sprints. This approach enables organizations to develop, test, and deploy new strategies swiftly, allowing for quick adaptation to new challenges and opportunities.

Incorporating customer feedback loops is crucial for maintaining relevance and alignment with market needs. Regularly collecting and acting upon customer feedback ensures that the organization's products and services continually meet and exceed market expectations.

Finally, continuous investment in technology and innovation is critical. By staying at the forefront of technological advancements and fostering a culture of innovation, organizations ensure they are well-equipped to adapt and thrive in an ever-evolving business landscape. This commitment to technology and innovation is a key differentiator for organizations led by visionary innovators.

MINDSETS ESSENTIAL FOR NAVIGATING CHANGE

In agile organizations, certain mindsets are pivotal for effective adaptation.

A core mindset is embracing change as the norm. Leaders in these organizations foster a culture where change is viewed not as a disruption but as an inherent part of the business landscape and an opportunity for growth. This approach helps teams navigate transitions with positivity and openness.

Fostering a culture of continuous learning is essential. Agile organizations encourage their employees to constantly update their skills and knowledge, keeping pace with rapid technological advancements and shifting market dynamics.

Promoting agility and flexibility is more than just a procedural aspect; it's a way of thinking. Leaders in these organizations instill a mindset of adaptability in their teams, encouraging them to be ready to pivot and adjust their approaches as necessary.

Encouraging experimentation and innovation is crucial. Creating an environment where trial and error are welcomed and where failures are viewed as valuable learning experiences fosters innovation and keeps the organization at the cutting edge of adaptability.

Valuing diverse perspectives is key to understanding and adapting to a multifaceted business environment. Leaders ensure that various viewpoints are not only sought but also highly valued, recognizing that diversity in thought leads to richer, more comprehensive strategies.

Developing resilience is fundamental. Visionary leaders focus on building organizational resilience, enabling the company to withstand market fluctuations and embrace the challenges that come with rapid change. This resilience is cultivated not just at an organizational level but also individually, within each team member.

CHAPTER 7
THE POWER OF
STRATEGIC FOCUS

IN AN AGE where distractions are incessant and multifaceted, the ability to maintain an intense focus on strategic objectives is what often sets visionary leaders apart. By examining the techniques these leaders employ, we can understand how they stay concentrated on core goals amidst a myriad of potential distractions. This skill transcends personal discipline; it's a strategic imperative that permeates their leadership style and the entire organizational ethos.

A prime example of this can be seen in the leadership approach of Satya Nadella at Microsoft. Upon assuming the role of CEO, Nadella swiftly refocused the company's efforts on cloud computing and AI, areas he identified as key to future growth. Despite the diverse range of Microsoft's interests, Nadella's clear vision and focused leadership have been instrumental in keeping the company aligned and concentrated on these new strategic goals, leading to significant growth in these areas.

His ability to filter out distractions and focus on strategic objectives exemplifies the importance of maintaining a clear and consistent vision, not just for individual leaders but for the entire organization. This focused approach under Nadella's leadership has been pivotal in reestablishing Microsoft as a leader in innovation and technology.

CULTIVATING A DISCIPLINE OF FOCUS

No leader rises to the top of his market without an exceptional ability to filter out noise and focus intensely on a few key objectives. Jobs, for instance, was famous for his focused product strategy, often emphasizing the importance of simplicity and clarity in both product design and corporate strategy. He believed in doing a few things exceptionally well rather than spreading efforts thinly over multiple fronts.

The key here is establishing priorities and providing clarity on goals. The ability to discern the essential tasks that align with the organization's long-term vision enables these leaders to filter out irrelevant projects. This clarity of purpose is a guiding light for all organizational activities.

In their quest for effectiveness, these leaders create environments conducive to deep, focused work. This can involve workspace designs that minimize distractions and foster concentration, as well as fostering a culture that respects and values focused time.

A critical aspect of maintaining focus is the ability to set and communicate clear boundaries. Visionary leaders define the scope of their organization's activities, clearly outlining the projects and initiatives they will not engage in. This firm stance helps maintain a straight course toward the organization's goals.

Technology is used strategically by these leaders. Rather than allowing it to become a distraction, they leverage tools like project management software and data analytics to enhance focus and keep track of essential performance metrics.

Regular strategic reviews are a staple in these organizations. These reviews help ensure that all activities remain aligned with core objectives, allowing for timely adjustments and realignments whenever focus shifts or deviates.

Empowering teams to maintain focus is key. By clearly defining roles, responsibilities, and expectations, leaders enable their teams to confidently decline tasks that fall outside their primary objectives, ensuring a concerted effort towards achieving the set goals.

In the journey to maintain strategic focus, saying 'no' is often more powerful than saying 'yes.' The critical role of declination is essential in upholding an organization's focus. Visionary leaders master the art of turning down opportunities that don't align with their vision.

PRIORITIZING STRATEGIC ALIGNMENT OVER OPPORTUNITY

The instinct to capitalize on every opportunity can lead to a dilution of effort and a drift away from core objectives. Visionary leaders, such as Amazon's Jeff Bezos, recognize that not every opportunity is the right opportunity. Bezos is known for his disciplined approach to opportunities, often passing up short-term gains to stay aligned with Amazon's long-term strategic vision, particularly in the realm of customer experience and innovation.

DETERMINING WHAT TO DECLINE

Visionary leaders meticulously align potential opportunities with their organization's core values and mission. They consider whether an opportunity reinforces these fundamental elements, declining those that don't align.

Long-term impact is a crucial consideration. They evaluate how an opportunity might influence their strategic goals over time, steering clear of those that could have negative long-term effects or don't significantly contribute to these objectives.

Resource allocation is another key factor. Leaders assess whether pursuing an opportunity might stretch their organization's resources or detract from more critical initiatives. They give priority to opportunities that make optimal use of the organization's assets without overextending its capabilities.

Risk versus reward is carefully balanced. Opportunities that present high risks without proportional rewards or that could compromise key strategic initiatives are often turned down.

Finally, decision-making is a collaborative process. Leaders don't operate in a vacuum; they seek insights from their teams and stakeholders, ensuring a comprehensive understanding of the opportunity at hand before making a decision. This collaborative approach ensures that all angles are considered, leading to well-informed, strategic decisions.

CULTIVATING A CULTURE OF STRATEGIC 'NO'

The most effective strategists actively foster a culture where it is not only acceptable but encouraged to decline tasks or projects when they detract from primary objectives. This empowerment instills a sense of ownership and accountability among team members.

Transparent communication is key in this approach. Leaders clearly explain the reasons behind turning down certain opportunities, ensuring that team members understand and are in sync with the organization's strategic focus. This openness helps build trust and clarity within the team.

Celebrating focused successes is also a part of this culture. When the decision to say 'no' leads to significant achievements, these successes are highlighted and celebrated. This practice reinforces the importance and value of maintaining strategic focus and the positive outcomes it can yield.

Moreover, leaders invest in training and mentorship to enhance team members' ability to discern effectively. This guidance helps them recognize opportunities that align with the organization's strategic direction and those that do not, fostering better decision-making skills within the team.

FOCUSING ON CORE STRENGTHS

One recurring theme in environments presided by great leaders is emphasis on the relentless enhancement and nurturing of an organization's core strengths. This process begins with a meticulous evaluation of the organization's distinctive capabilities—identifying its strongest suits and competitive edge. Leaders delve into the analysis of past successes, market positioning, and internal competencies to understand these unique strengths.

Leveraging customer feedback and thorough market analysis to grasp what clients and the broader market value most is pivotal in identifying areas where the organization excels and should persistently focus its efforts.

In aligning these core strengths with market needs and trends, visionaries ensure their organizational focus is not only on areas of proficiency but also on fulfilling significant market demands. They seek the convergence point where their top capabilities intersect with substantial market needs.

To maintain and elevate these strengths, visionary leaders commit to ongoing improvement. This commitment manifests in various forms, such as investing in training, research and development, or integrating new technologies that augment these pivotal capabilities. The goal is to continuously refine and bolster what the organization does best, ensuring it stays ahead in a competitive landscape.

AVOIDING FRAGMENTATION OF GOALS

Visionary leaders emphasize clear strategic prioritization, focusing on enhancing and expanding their organization's core strengths. They steer clear of opportunities that don't align with these critical areas. To ensure alignment throughout the organization, these leaders consistently communicate the importance of these core focus areas, making sure that every team and employee understands and aligns with these priorities.

They further reinforce this focus by implementing reward systems that recognize and incentivize efforts and achievements in the organization's areas of strength. This approach ensures that employees are motivated to concentrate their efforts where they matter most.

To maintain this strategic alignment, regular strategic reviews must be conducted. These reviews serve to confirm that the organization remains steadfast in its focus on core strengths and does not stray into less impactful or divergent areas. This disciplined approach to strategic focus ensures the organization stays on course, capitalizing on its unique capabilities to achieve long-term success.

BALANCING CORE STRENGTHS WITH ADAPTABILITY

Leadership mastery relies on the ability to focus on core strengths while maintaining adaptability. Visionaries maintain flexibility in how these core strengths are applied, ensuring the organization can swiftly adapt to changing market conditions. This approach ensures the organization's foundational capabilities are not just static assets but dynamic tools that respond effectively to the evolving business landscape.

At the same time, these leaders foster innovation within their areas of core strength. This strategy ensures that these capabilities continue to evolve, maintaining their relevance and competitive edge. By encouraging innovation within their foundational areas, visionary leaders ensure that their organizations remain at the forefront of their industries, continually adapting and improving.

MAINTAINING FOCUS DURING ORGANIZATIONAL GROWTH

As organizations expand, visionary leaders understand the importance of maintaining a strategic focus, ensuring that growth aligns with core objectives and values. They begin by frequently revisiting and reaffirming the organization's core values, ensuring these principles remain central to decision-making and strategic direction, even during periods of rapid expansion.

Scalable strategic planning is critical in this phase. These leaders devise plans that are both adaptable and flexible, accommodating growth while staying aligned with long-term goals and vision. Clear communication channels are established to ensure all employees, whether longstanding or new, are well-informed and in sync with the organization's focus.

Developing strong leadership across various organizational levels is another key strategy. This approach decentralizes decision-making yet keeps it aligned with the organization's core objectives and values. Leaders at different tiers are empowered to make decisions that adhere to these central principles.

Continuous monitoring and alignment checks are fundamental. Leaders regularly assess whether growth initiatives and new ventures align with the organization's primary focus. They ensure that every step towards expansion is in harmony with the established strategic path.

Cultivating a culture of consistency is essential, especially as the organization grows. This culture, steeped in the organization's core values and focus areas, is integrated into every aspect of the organization, from onboarding new hires to day-to-day operations. This approach ensures that despite the challenges of scaling, the organization's strategic focus remains undiluted and clear.

BALANCING EXPANSION WITH STRATEGIC FOCUS

It's critical to develop the ability to navigate the delicate balance between pursuing growth and maintaining strategic focus. To be an effective leader, you must prioritize quality over quantity, ensuring that every aspect of expansion, be it product development, market entry, or talent acquisition, adheres to the organization's high standards and aligns with its overarching goals.

Selective about growth opportunities, iconic leaders choose paths that best resonate with the organization's strategic objectives and core competencies. They understand that not all opportunities are equal and that discernment is key to sustainable growth.

Central to their approach is an unwavering focus on customer-centricity. Even amidst expansion, they ensure the organization never loses sight of its customers' needs and expectations, recognizing this as the foundation of their initial success.

Even more importantly, they foster a culture of agility and adaptability within their teams. By encouraging this mindset, they ensure the organization remains nimble and focused, capable of growing and adapting to new challenges without straying from its strategic path. This approach allows for growth that is not only rapid but also sustainable and aligned with the company's long-term vision.

ALIGNING TEAM FOCUS WITH ORGANIZATIONAL GOALS

Visionary leaders adeptly navigate the challenge of keeping every team within their organization aligned and focused on overarching strategic goals. They understand the importance of ensuring that all teams, irrespective of their specific functions or projects, contribute cohesively towards the central objectives.

To achieve this, they emphasize clear and consistent communication of the organization's strategic goals. This involves not just announcing these goals but also articulating their importance and explaining how each team's efforts contribute to them. Regular strategic alignment meetings are a staple in their approach, providing a forum for teams to discuss and ensure their work is in sync with the organization's broader aims.

They skillfully integrate these strategic goals into team and individual performance metrics, making the achievement of these objectives a core responsibility of each team. This approach aligns individual performance with organizational success, creating a direct link between daily activities and strategic objectives.

Encouraging cross-functional collaboration is another key strategy. By fostering collaborations across different departments, they break down silos and encourage a unified approach to achieving organizational goals.

These collaborations often provide fresh perspectives and enhance overall strategic alignment.

Investment in leadership training and development across all levels is pivotal. This training equips team leaders with the necessary skills in strategic planning, communication, and team management, ensuring they can effectively guide their teams in alignment with the organization's goals.

Lastly, they establish mechanisms for regular feedback from teams regarding their alignment with organizational goals. This feedback is crucial for assessing effectiveness and making necessary adjustments, ensuring that the organization remains agile and responsive to both internal and external shifts.

PRACTICES FOR MAINTAINING FOCUS ON CENTRAL OBJECTIVES

Visionary leaders skillfully set clear and measurable objectives for each team, ensuring these objectives align with the organization's overarching strategic goals. This approach provides teams with a focused direction, channeling their efforts toward the most impactful areas.

They strike a balance between autonomy and guidance, empowering teams with the freedom to operate independently while ensuring their actions remain within frameworks that support the organization's strategic direction. This autonomy is complemented by ensuring that resources—be it budget, time, or personnel—are strategically allocated, particularly to teams working on key strategic areas. Such targeted resource allocation underscores the importance of these areas and ensures that crucial projects have the necessary support to succeed.

A culture of accountability is deeply ingrained, where teams are held responsible for their contributions towards these strategic goals. This culture not only reinforces the significance of these goals but also maintains a sharp focus across the organization.

Furthermore, leaders celebrate and publicly recognize achievements that are in line with organizational goals. This act of celebration not only acknowledges the hard work and success of teams but also serves as a powerful motivator, encouraging continued focus and alignment with the organization's objectives.

BALANCING LONG-TERM VISION WITH IMMEDIATE GOALS

Visionary leaders masterfully align short-term objectives with their long-term visions, ensuring that each immediate goal contributes meaningfully to the larger picture. They map out the path from present actions to future achievements, creating coherence and alignment in all organizational efforts.

Their strategic planning approach is both robust and flexible, allowing for the adaptation of short-term plans to meet immediate challenges or opportunities, all while keeping the long-term vision firmly in view. This dynamic approach ensures resilience and relevance in a rapidly changing business environment.

Effective communication is a cornerstone of their leadership. They consistently articulate the long-term vision and clarify how short-term goals fit into this broader framework. This ongoing communication ensures that everyone in the organization understands and remains committed to both immediate tasks and future objectives.

Prioritization and resource allocation are handled with a keen eye, balancing immediate operational needs with long-term ambitions. Visionary leaders often face tough choices about where to focus energy and resources, decisions they navigate by weighing short-term benefits against long-term gains.

Regular review and realignment processes are integral to their strategy. These processes involve assessing both short-term achievements and progress towards the long-term vision. Such reviews allow for the realignment of strategies and objectives as necessary, ensuring that the organization stays on track toward its ultimate goals.

ENSURING SHORT-TERM OBJECTIVES FEED INTO THE BROADER VISION

Visionary leaders skillfully navigate the path to their long-term vision by setting strategic short-term milestones. These milestones are thoughtfully crafted to gradually build towards the overarching vision, ensuring each step is purposeful and aligned with the end goal.

They embed feedback loops within their organizational processes. These loops facilitate continuous learning from short-term outcomes, allowing for adjustments and refinements in strategy as they progress toward their long-term vision.

Innovation is woven into the fabric of day-to-day operations under their leadership. This approach ensures that routine work not only meets immediate needs but also contributes to broader strategic objectives. They create an environment where innovative thinking is the norm, even in the smallest tasks.

Balancing agility with consistency is a hallmark of their strategy. They maintain flexibility to respond to immediate demands while ensuring that each action remains consistent with the path to the long-term vision. This balance is critical in adapting to present challenges without losing sight of future goals.

The cultivation of a forward-thinking organizational culture is central to their leadership. In this culture, employees are encouraged to consider the future implications of their daily work. This fosters a mindset among the workforce that naturally aligns short-term actions with the long-term vision, creating a cohesive journey towards the ultimate goals of the organization.

CHAPTER 8
INSPIRING PEOPLE AROUND A VISION

AT THE HEART of visionary leadership lies the ability to paint a compelling and vivid picture of the future. The techniques these leaders use to not only envision a transformative future but also communicate it in a way that captivates and aligns their teams towards a common goal are crucial in inspiring people to embrace the journey ahead and work collectively towards the realization of a shared vision.

A prime example of this can be found in the leadership of Shantanu Narayen at Adobe. Under Narayen's vision, Adobe transformed from a traditional software company to a leader in digital creativity and marketing software.

Narayen's ability to articulate a future where creativity and digital experience are paramount has been central to Adobe's strategic direction. He communicated this vision through consistent messaging, aligning product development, marketing, and corporate strategy around this core concept.

This vision was not just a distant dream; it was made tangible through Adobe's innovative product line, reflecting the future Narayen envisioned. By articulating this clear and compelling vision, Narayen has been able to align his team towards a common goal, leading Adobe through significant industry shifts and technological advancements. His leadership exemplifies how a well-communicated vision can inspire and mobilize an entire organization toward transformative success.

CRAFTING AND COMMUNICATING A COMPELLING VISION

Leaders like Elon Musk exemplify the power of articulating a clear and inspiring vision. Musk's vision for SpaceX—making life multi-planetary—transcends a mere corporate goal; it's a compelling narrative that captivates and motivates both his team and the wider public.

These leaders excel in using storytelling to bring their visions to life. They craft narratives that are not only relatable but also deeply engaging, employing vivid imagery and personal anecdotes. This approach makes the future they envision more tangible and connects deeply with the aspirations and values of their audience.

They skillfully link the organizational vision to a broader, more meaningful purpose. This alignment illustrates how realizing the vision will create a significant impact that extends beyond the company's immediate interests. This deeper sense of purpose galvanizes teams, inspiring them to strive harder and reach further.

The personal passion and belief a leader holds in their vision can be incredibly influential. Leaders who show authentic enthusiasm and unwavering commitment to their vision tend to inspire similar fervor in their teams. This shared passion becomes the driving force behind the collective effort to turn the vision into reality.

ALIGNING YOUR TEAM AROUND THE VISION

Visionary leaders actively engage in interactive dialogues with their teams, inviting questions and discussions about the vision. This open, two-way communication helps not only to clarify and refine the vision but also to reinforce its importance and relevance.

They skillfully connect each team member's role and contributions to the achievement of the vision. This connection helps individuals see how their efforts contribute to the larger goals, making the vision more tangible and personally relevant to them.

By involving teams in developing and shaping the vision and valuing their input, leaders foster a sense of ownership and inclusivity. This approach makes team members feel they are integral parts of a larger mission, which is crucial for sustaining collective motivation and commitment.

Consistent reinforcement of the vision within an

organization should be among any visionary's top priorities. This is achieved by integrating the vision into regular communications, creating visual reminders, and weaving the vision into the fabric of organizational rituals and practices. This constant presence keeps the vision at the forefront of organizational life, guiding and inspiring continuous effort toward its realization.

LEADING WITH PASSION AND CONVICTION

In the world of transformative leadership, the passion and conviction of a leader play a pivotal role in motivating and inspiring teams. If you harness your enthusiasm and believe in your vision, those around you will catch that infectious spark. With his passion for innovation, Richard Branson of the Virgin Group has been a driving force behind Virgin's ventures into new domains, from music to space travel, illustrating the power of a leader's energy in galvanizing a team.

Leaders who exude passion and conviction energize their teams. Their enthusiasm serves as a powerful motivator, spurring teams to tackle challenges with positivity and determination. This energy is crucial in building a shared sense of purpose and excitement.

Moreover, when leaders demonstrate unwavering belief in their vision, it instills trust and confidence in their teams. This conviction reassures team members of the leader's commitment and the feasibility of the vision, encouraging a collective belief in the goals ahead.

Passionate leaders also shape compelling workplace cultures. They foster environments that are dynamic, enthusiastic, and driven, which not only attract talent but also retain it. Such cultures provide a stimulating and rewarding work environment where team members feel part of something significant and fulfilling.

IMPACT OF A LEADER'S ENTHUSIASM ON TEAM MOTIVATION

A leader's enthusiasm for their vision plays a crucial role in inspiring teams to fully commit to their roles, often translating into perseverance, especially during challenging times. This unwavering commitment, fostered by the leader's passion, helps teams stay the course and push through setbacks.

Such passionate leaders create an environment where creativity and innovation naturally thrive. Their excitement and openness to new ideas encourage team members to think innovatively, bringing forward unique and creative solutions. This atmosphere of innovation is vital for fostering growth and evolution within the team.

The positive energy emanating from an enthusiastic leader significantly enhances team morale and engagement. When team members observe their leader's deep investment in the vision, it often heightens their own engagement and job satisfaction, creating a more vibrant and productive workplace.

Moreover, passionate leaders often act as role models, demonstrating how to approach work with zeal and a positive outlook. Their behavior sets a powerful example, influencing the organizational climate and team dynamics profoundly. This modeling of positive behavior is instrumental in shaping a healthy, dynamic work culture that values enthusiasm and a can-do attitude.

BALANCING PASSION WITH PRACTICAL LEADERSHIP

Visionary leaders skillfully balance their passion and conviction with practical leadership qualities, ensuring a well-rounded and effective approach.

Firstly, they exhibit a grounded optimism, blending their enthusiasm with a realistic understanding of the practical challenges and constraints they face. This approach ensures that their passion is rooted in the realities of their situation, enabling them to navigate obstacles more effectively and set achievable goals.

Secondly, these leaders practice inclusive leadership. They recognize the importance of ensuring that their fervor does not overshadow or suppress the ideas and contributions of their team members. Instead, they use their enthusiasm to foster an inclusive environment where every voice is heard and valued. This inclusive approach not only encourages diverse perspectives but also ensures that the team feels valued and integral to the organization's success.

EFFECTIVE COMMUNICATION FOR SHARED MISSIONS

Visionary leaders excel in communicating a shared mission, utilizing specific strategies and frameworks to not only convey their vision but also to inspire and unify their teams around it. They recognize the profound impact that effective communication has on how the mission resonates and motivates.

To start with, these leaders prioritize clarity and consistency in their communication. They express the mission in simple, straightforward language, avoiding jargon and complexity. This approach ensures that team members clearly understand the mission and their role within it.

Another key tactic is storytelling. Leaders use storytelling to make the mission more relatable and engaging. By sharing narratives that encompass challenges, triumphs, and the journey, they enable team members to connect with the mission on a more personal level.

Emotional connection is also vital. Leaders communicate in a manner that fosters an emotional bond with the team. By sharing their own passion and commitment to the mission, they make it more relatable, thereby inspiring team members to embrace and follow it.

Effective communication is a two-way street. Leaders promote active participation by inviting feedback and ideas from team members, enhancing engagement, and fostering a stronger connection to the mission.

Visual and symbolic communication also play a

crucial role. Visionary leaders often employ visual aids and symbols, such as logos and infographics, to continually reinforce the mission. These visual elements act as persistent reminders of the shared purpose, uniting the team in pursuit of common goals.

FRAMEWORKS FOR INSPIRING AROUND THE MISSION

Regular mission-centric meetings and forums are key in reinforcing the organizational mission and engaging the team. These gatherings provide a platform for sharing progress updates, discussing challenges, and celebrating achievements that align with the mission. They are essential for keeping the team focused and connected to the organization's overarching goals.

Leadership messaging plays a critical role in this process. Every form of communication from the leadership, be it internal memos, public addresses, or casual conversations, consistently echoes the mission. This consistent alignment ensures that the mission is woven into the fabric of all organizational communication, keeping it at the forefront of every team member's mind.

Training and development initiatives are also closely tied to the mission. By aligning these programs with the organizational goals, leaders ensure that team members are equipped with the necessary skills and knowledge to effectively contribute to the mission. This alignment is crucial for building a competent and mission-driven workforce.

Moreover, the implementation of recognition and reward systems that applaud efforts towards achieving the mission plays a significant role in reinforcing its importance. Such systems motivate team members to align their efforts with the organizational goals, contributing to a unified and focused pursuit of the mission.

CULTIVATING PASSIONATE DEVOTEES OF THE VISION

Visionary leaders excel at crafting an environment where team members become deeply committed to the organization's vision. This dedicated culture is vital for propelling an organization towards its objectives, fostering a sense of purpose and dedication that transcends standard job responsibilities.

One key method they use is leading by example, living the vision through their actions and decisions. Like Howard Schultz of Starbucks, who consistently championed quality and social responsibility, they become role models, inspiring others to embody the organization's values and goals.

These leaders also employ inspirational leadership techniques that motivate and uplift their team members. Their communication style is not just informative but also energizing, helping the team to feel part of something greater than themselves.

Creating emotional connections between the team and the vision is another cornerstone of their approach.

They craft compelling narratives around the vision that resonate with team members on a personal level, turning the vision into a collective aspiration.

Team members are empowered when higher-ups give them autonomy in their roles. This empowerment allows individuals to take ownership of their part in realizing the vision, fostering a personal connection and passion for the organizational goals. This autonomy is crucial in allowing team members to discover and nurture their unique contributions to the vision.

KEY ELEMENTS IN FOSTERING A DEDICATED CULTURE

Visionary leaders excel in maintaining the relevance and prominence of their vision through clear and consistent communication. By frequently articulating the vision and its importance, they ensure it stays central in the team's collective consciousness, with consistent messaging underscoring its significance.

They adeptly align individual team members' goals and career aspirations with the organization's overarching vision, helping each person see how their personal development is intertwined with the collective progress towards these goals.

Acknowledging and celebrating contributions that advance the vision is a key strategy. These leaders celebrate both individual and team achievements, fostering an ongoing sense of enthusiasm and commitment toward the shared objectives.

Creating shared experiences that relate to the vision, such as team-building exercises, volunteering projects, or company-wide initiatives, further solidifies the team's bond with the vision. These activities enhance the sense of unity and purpose among team members.

Encouraging innovation and creativity is another essential aspect of their leadership. They create an environment where team members can freely propose ideas and innovations that bolster the vision, fostering a sense of ownership and keeping the vision dynamic and progressive.

Their use of emotional intelligence is pivotal. They connect with their team members on a deeper level, understanding and addressing their motivations, challenges, and aspirations in relation to the organizational vision. This empathetic approach helps in nurturing a team that is deeply invested in and aligned with the vision's fulfillment.

EMBEDDING THE VISION IN ORGANIZATIONAL CULTURE

Visionary leaders excel in making their vision a tangible and active part of their organization's culture. Their vision transcends being merely a statement and becomes a guiding force in everyday operations and interactions.

One of their key strategies is the constant communication of the vision. They weave the vision into various aspects of organizational life—from formal meetings and internal communications to casual workplace conversations. This ongoing reinforcement ensures that the vision remains a focal point in everyone's daily activities.

Aligning organizational policies, procedures, and guidelines with the vision is another crucial step. These leaders ensure every aspect of the organization reflects and supports the vision, emphasizing its relevance in all facets of operations.

Training and development programs are carefully crafted to mirror the vision's principles and goals. New employees are introduced to these concepts from their first day, and ongoing development efforts consistently reinforce the vision's core principles.

Notably, they incorporate the vision into performance metrics. Performance evaluations include criteria that assess contributions to the vision, motivating employees to align their efforts with these overarching goals in quantifiable ways. This approach ensures that working towards the vision is not just aspirational but is embedded in the practical, measurable aspects of their roles.

CULTURAL RITUALS AND PRACTICES THAT REINFORCE THE VISION

Visionary leaders implement various strategies to ensure their vision is deeply ingrained in the culture and daily operations of their organization.

They establish meaningful rituals and celebrations that focus on the vision. These can range from annual events commemorating key milestones to regular team meetings that celebrate achievements tied to the vision. These events reinforce the vision's importance and keep it at the forefront of everyone's mind.

Storytelling becomes a key tool in making the vision come alive. Leaders share success stories, customer testimonials, and experiences from employees that illustrate the vision in action. This approach makes the vision relatable and engaging, creating a narrative that employees can connect with.

Recognition programs are carefully aligned with the vision. These systems are designed to acknowledge and reward individuals and teams who demonstrate the vision through their work, thereby reinforcing its centrality to the organization's success.

Leaders themselves play a crucial role by acting as role models. They embody the vision in their own actions and decisions, setting a powerful example for others in the organization to follow.

Physical reminders of the vision are strategically placed throughout the workplace. This could be in the form of posters, digital displays, and other visual cues, serving as constant reinforcements of the vision and its significance.

Involving employees in the development and evolution of the vision is also a key tactic. Leaders seek input and feedback from their teams, making the vision a collaborative and inclusive process. This involvement fosters a sense of ownership and deeper commitment among employees.

Leaders make a concerted effort to link the vision to everyday activities. They help employees understand how their daily tasks contribute to the broader vision, making it relevant and meaningful to each individual role within the organization. This approach ensures that the vision is more than just a statement; it's a living, breathing part of the organization's daily life.

EMPOWERING TEAMS TO CHAMPION THE VISION

Visionary leaders employ several strategies to empower their teams and align them with the organization's vision.

Firstly, they delegate authority, placing trust in their teams to make decisions that are in line with the organization's vision. This delegation is not just a transfer of tasks but a sign of confidence in the team's capabilities and judgment. It empowers team members, giving them the autonomy to take initiative and act as proactive ambassadors of the vision.

Secondly, these leaders ensure that their teams are well-equipped with the necessary resources, training, and support to effectively champion the vision. They provide access to critical information, the latest tools, and ample opportunities for team members to develop skills that are directly relevant to achieving the vision.

This level of support is vital for teams to feel confident and capable in their roles.

Lastly, visionary leaders create and encourage the use of platforms for idea-sharing and innovation. These could be in the form of regular team meetings, specialized innovation workshops, or digital forums designed to facilitate the exchange of ideas. These platforms become crucial spaces where teams can collaboratively contribute to the vision, sharing their insights, innovations, and strategies that align with and further the organizational goals.

ENCOURAGING INITIATIVE AND OWNERSHIP

Visionary leaders employ several effective strategies to ensure their teams are aligned with and actively contributing to the organization's vision. They set clear expectations and goals that are directly related to the vision. This approach provides teams and individuals with a tangible roadmap, guiding them in how they can contribute effectively to the organization's overarching objectives. These clear goals help team members understand their role in the larger picture and how their work directly impacts the realization of the vision.

These leaders place a strong emphasis on recognizing and celebrating the contributions that further the organization's vision. By acknowledging and appreciating efforts that align with and advance the vision, leaders reinforce its significance. This recognition serves as a powerful motivation for teams and individuals, encouraging them to continue their efforts toward championing the vision.

They encourage and facilitate cross-departmental collaboration. By breaking down silos and promoting interdepartmental cooperation, leaders foster a wider spread of the vision across the organization. This approach creates a network of advocates for the vision, ensuring that it is embraced and advanced by all parts of the organization.

And lastly, visionary leaders incorporate aspects of the vision into individual personal development plans. This integration ensures that each employee's growth and development are aligned with the broader goals of the organization. It helps team members see the value in developing skills and capabilities that not only benefit their personal career trajectories but also contribute significantly to achieving the organization's vision.

EMPOWERING TEAMS TO EXTERNALIZE THE VISION

Visionary leaders adopt several key strategies to ensure that their teams are not just aligned with, but also actively promoting the organization's vision both internally and externally. They foster engagement with the wider community and industry. Leaders encourage their teams to actively participate in external events like industry conferences, community activities, or through social media engagement. This external engagement serves a dual purpose—it helps spread the vision beyond the confines of the organization, and it also allows team members to see the broader impact of their work.

They place a strong emphasis on developing leadership skills within the teams. By investing in training and mentorship programs, leaders ensure that there are multiple advocates capable of articulately and passionately advancing the vision. This development of internal leadership is crucial for ensuring that the vision is communicated effectively and consistently.

Visionary leaders work to cultivate a sense of collective mission within their teams. This is more than just having a shared goal; it's about fostering a deep sense of belonging and purpose, where every team member feels they are part of something larger than themselves. This sense of collective mission is a powerful motivator for team members to actively promote and work towards the vision, as it aligns with their personal values and aspirations.

CHAPTER 9
EXECUTING A STRATEGIC MASTERPLAN

VISIONARY LEADERS APPROACH the execution of strategic plans with a level of precision and meticulousness that can be likened to military operations. This approach is characterized by careful planning, rigorous execution, and constant monitoring, ensuring that every aspect of the plan is executed with utmost efficiency and effectiveness.

One real-world example of this approach can be seen in the leadership style of Tim Cook at Apple Inc. Since taking over as CEO, Cook has been known for his meticulous attention to detail and operational efficiency. Under his leadership, Apple has seen the precise execution of strategic initiatives, such as the expansion into new markets with products like the Apple Watch and services like Apple Music and Apple Pay.

Cook's focus on the seamless integration of Apple's supply chain and operations has been critical in realizing these ambitious projects. This precision in execution has helped Apple continue its legacy of innovation, maintaining its position as a technology leader. By following a methodical approach to strategic execution, Cook has demonstrated how precision and attention to detail are pivotal in transforming ambitious visions into tangible, successful realities.

METHODICAL APPROACH TO STRATEGIC EXECUTION

Visionary leaders approach the execution of their strategies with meticulous planning and a comprehensive approach. They start by laying out detailed plans, breaking down the overarching strategy into specific, manageable components. These plans are supported by clearly defined roadmaps, which delineate timelines, key actions, and the responsibilities of various parties involved.

To ensure the effectiveness of each stage of their plan, they set clear objectives and establish success metrics. These metrics are chosen for their relevance and ability to accurately reflect progress toward achieving the set goals. Monitoring these metrics is a critical part of the process, involving regular check-ins and control mechanisms to ensure that every aspect of the plan unfolds as intended.

Efficient and strategic allocation of resources is a cornerstone of their approach. Visionary leaders ensure that every element of the plan, from personnel to finances to technology, has the necessary resources for successful implementation.

Understanding that no plan is immune to risks and challenges, they incorporate risk management and contingency planning into their strategy. By anticipating potential obstacles and preparing for them, they equip their organizations to respond swiftly and effectively to unforeseen challenges, minimizing any potential disruptions to the plan's progression. This thorough and proactive approach is fundamental to the precise and effective execution of their strategic vision.

ENSURING METICULOUS AND EFFICIENT EXECUTION

Forward-thinking pioneers utilize a variety of methods to ensure the meticulous execution of their strategies. Key to this approach is maintaining open and frequent communication throughout the organization. This ongoing dialogue ensures that everyone understands their role and the importance of their contributions to the strategic objectives.

Leaders at various levels are empowered with the autonomy to make decisions and manage their teams, aligning with the strategic plan. This empowerment fosters a sense of ownership and responsibility, which is crucial for precise execution. Understanding that conditions can change, these leaders are committed to flexibility. Regular reviews of the plan's progress are conducted, allowing for necessary adjustments to keep the plan on track and relevant.

Additionally, a culture of accountability is cultivated within the organization. In this environment, every team member knows the value of their role and is committed to executing their part of the plan with precision. This culture of accountability and clear communication ensures that the strategic plan is not only understood across all levels of the organization but also effectively and accurately implemented.

SYSTEMATIC ACHIEVEMENT OF MILESTONES

Futuristic strategists in pursuit of audacious goals adopt a systematic approach to reaching milestones, a key element examined in Chapter 9. This section delves into the techniques these leaders use to methodically achieve each milestone while maintaining momentum, particularly in the face of challenges. They start by breaking down large, audacious goals into smaller, more manageable milestones. This segmentation renders the goals less daunting and provides clear, achievable targets for teams.

For each milestone, specific and realistic yet challenging timelines are established, injecting a sense of urgency and focus. To keep track of progress towards these milestones, leaders implement systems for regular tracking and reporting. This could involve the use of dashboards, regular meetings, or progress reports, ensuring everyone is informed and accountable.

Advanced project management tools and software are employed to streamline coordination efforts, track progress, and manage resources effectively. These tools offer a transparent view of where teams stand in relation to their designated milestones, aiding in efficient and targeted efforts towards achieving the set objectives.

MAINTAINING MOMENTUM AMIDST CHALLENGES

Visionary leaders employ various techniques to maintain momentum, particularly in the face of obstacles. They foster an environment conducive to adaptive problem-solving, where teams are encouraged to rapidly identify issues, brainstorm solutions, and pivot strategies as needed. To keep the team motivated, they engage in inspirational leadership, consistently reminding teams of the larger goals, celebrating incremental successes, and providing ongoing encouragement and support.

These leaders are adept at quickly reallocating resources or offering additional support where necessary to navigate challenges and stay on course toward their milestones. They also establish efficient feedback loops, enabling the prompt collection and integration of feedback. This feedback is critical in making timely adjustments to strategies and approaches, ensuring that the path to achieving milestones is continually optimized and responsive to evolving circumstances.

ENSURING ALIGNMENT WITH OVERALL GOALS

Throughout their journey of reaching milestones, visionary leaders take meticulous steps to ensure that these milestones are in harmony with the organization's overarching goals. They meticulously align each milestone with the strategic objectives of the organization, making certain that every advancement contributes meaningfully towards the larger aspirations.

Leaders also emphasize the importance of each milestone to their teams, consistently reinforcing the critical role these accomplishments play in the context of the broader objectives. By celebrating the achievement of these milestones, leaders not only bolster morale but also underscore the progress being made towards these overarching goals. These celebrations act as tangible reminders of the team's collective journey and the strides being taken toward realizing the vision.

ADAPTING AND DOUBLING DOWN

In the dynamic landscape of executing strategic plans, visionary leaders often grapple with the delicate balance between steadfastness and adaptability. Their leadership is characterized by a keen awareness of when to firmly uphold their strategies and when to embrace change, adapting their tactics in response to new information or evolving circumstances.

Central to this balance is the continuous evaluation of the core assumptions underpinning their strategies. Leaders rigorously assess whether current data reinforces these assumptions, signaling a need to intensify efforts and invest further resources. Conversely, when foundational assumptions are challenged by new realities, they are poised to make strategic adjustments.

An integral part of this decision-making process involves a vigilant monitoring of market feedback. Insights gleaned from customers, competitive analysis, and industry trends are meticulously analyzed to determine the efficacy of existing strategies. This external feedback serves as a critical barometer for whether to maintain the course or pivot.

Additionally, the interpretation of performance metrics plays a crucial role. These objective indicators can signal the success or faltering of current strategies. Positive trends in these metrics might encourage leaders to amplify their efforts, while negative trends could prompt a thorough reassessment and realignment of strategies. This nuanced approach allows visionary leaders to navigate the complex interplay of staying true to their vision while remaining agile and responsive to the ever-changing business landscape.

DECISION-MAKING FOR DOUBLING DOWN OR ADAPTING

In navigating strategic decisions, visionary leaders employ a meticulous approach, especially when contemplating intensifying their efforts in a particular direction. A crucial step in this process is conducting a comprehensive risk assessment to fully understand the implications of ramping up efforts. This assessment involves a careful analysis of potential risks versus expected benefits, aiding leaders in determining the most prudent path forward.

Scenario planning is another key tool in their decision-making arsenal. Leaders use this technique to forecast various outcomes of maintaining their current strategy versus adjusting it. This exploration includes delving into both best-case and worst-case scenarios, providing a well-rounded view of potential future states.

Collaboration and consultation form the cornerstone of their strategic deliberation process. Leaders engage with their leadership teams and draw on cross-functional insights, ensuring a broad and diverse perspective informs any significant strategic decisions.

Additionally, incremental testing plays a vital role. Before fully committing to a particular course of action, they often initiate small-scale tests to gauge the viability and potential success of increased investment in a strategy. This step-by-step approach allows them to validate their assumptions and fine-tune their strategies with a higher degree of confidence and lower risk.

ADJUSTING TACTICS WHEN NECESSARY

Visionary leaders embody agility in their leadership style, always ready to modify their tactics in response to new and relevant information that suggests a different approach might be more advantageous. This flexibility is a key trait that allows them to navigate the ever-changing business landscape effectively.

When shifts in strategy are required, these leaders excel in transparently communicating the rationale behind these changes. Clear and effective communication is crucial to ensure that the entire team understands, buys into, and aligns with the new direction. This transparency helps maintain trust and cohesion within the team, even amidst changes.

Understanding that the market is a dynamic and evolving entity, leaders who adjust their tactics do so with keen insights gleaned from market changes. They view these shifts not as setbacks but as valuable learning opportunities that can shape and refine future strategies.

Throughout these adjustments, they meticulously ensure that the new tactics remain aligned with the organization's broader strategic vision. This steadfast commitment to strategic coherence guarantees that, despite changes in tactics, all efforts continue to contribute effectively to the overarching goals and objectives of the organization.

FRAMEWORKS FOR STRATEGIC PLANNING

In the realm of visionary leadership, strategic planning is fundamental, and the adoption of various frameworks and models is pivotal in shaping and effectively executing a strategic vision. Visionary leaders utilize a blend of established and innovative frameworks to guide their strategy formulation and implementation.

The SWOT Analysis is a fundamental tool, allowing leaders to thoroughly assess their organization's internal strengths and weaknesses alongside external opportunities and threats. This comprehensive analysis lays the groundwork for pinpointing strategic priorities and developing actionable plans.

The Objectives and Key Results (OKRs) framework, which has gained popularity in leading companies like Google, is instrumental in setting clear, specific objectives paired with measurable results. OKRs foster organizational alignment and focus efforts on quantifiable outcomes, ensuring that everyone is working towards the same goals.

The Balanced Scorecard approach broadens the perspective beyond just financial metrics, taking into account customer satisfaction, efficiency of internal processes, and organizational learning and growth. This multidimensional view provides a more comprehensive understanding of success and progress.

Additionally, the Blue Ocean Strategy is particularly effective for visionary leaders looking to carve out new market spaces. This approach focuses on exploring and capitalizing on untapped market opportunities, steering clear of the intense competition in existing markets. By employing this strategy, leaders can discover and develop new avenues for growth and innovation.

GUIDANCE PROVIDED BY STRATEGIC PLANNING FRAMEWORKS

Visionary leadership relies heavily on strategic frameworks to guide and refine the direction of an organization. These frameworks serve as a compass, delineating the current position of the organization, charting the desired future destination, and mapping out the pathways to reach these goals. They play a crucial role in ensuring that every part of the organization, from various departments to individual teams, is harmoniously aligned with the common objectives, with a clear understanding of how their individual efforts contribute to the broader strategy.

These strategic frameworks are instrumental in streamlining decision-making processes. They provide a well-structured approach to evaluating different options and possible routes, thereby facilitating more informed and effective decisions. Moreover, some of these frameworks are specifically designed to enhance organizational agility, enabling a swift and adaptable response to external changes. This adaptability is key in maintaining the relevance and efficacy of the strategy amidst evolving market and environmental conditions. By leveraging these frameworks, visionary leaders can ensure that their strategies are not only well-defined but also flexible and responsive to the dynamic business landscape.

INTEGRATING FRAMEWORKS INTO ORGANIZATIONAL CULTURE

Visionary leaders deeply embed strategic planning frameworks into the organizational culture, ensuring that they're not just tools for planning but integral parts of the daily operations and mindset of the organization. A culture of regular strategic reviews is cultivated, where these frameworks are employed not just to chart progress but also to identify areas needing adjustment and refinement. This practice keeps the strategy dynamic and responsive to both internal and external changes.

Integral to this approach is the involvement of employees in the strategic planning process. Leaders actively engage team members across all levels in understanding and contributing to the strategic objectives. This inclusive approach not only fosters a deeper organizational commitment to these goals but also encourages a broader and richer pool of ideas and perspectives.

Moreover, there's a strong emphasis on continuous learning and development in strategic thinking. Leaders encourage teams to stay abreast of the latest models and trends in strategic planning, fostering an environment where learning is ongoing and directly tied to the strategic objectives of the organization. This approach ensures that the organization's strategic thinking evolves continuously, adapting to new challenges and opportunities in the business landscape.

COMMITMENT STRATEGIES FOR LONG-TERM GOALS

Visionary leaders adeptly employ commitment strategies to align their teams and maintain focus on the organization's long-term goals, a key aspect in the execution of any strategic plan. These strategies play a pivotal role in ensuring sustained effort and perseverance, particularly when traversing the complexities and challenges of long-term initiatives.

At the core of these strategies is the alignment of individual roles and responsibilities with the organization's vision. Leaders make it a priority to ensure that every team member understands how their work directly contributes to these long-term objectives. This understanding not only fosters a sense of purpose but also nurtures a deep-seated commitment to the shared goals.

Communication plays a critical role in keeping these long-term goals at the forefront of the team's mind. Through regular updates, meetings, and even informal interactions, leaders consistently reinforce the importance and progress of these objectives. This steady stream of communication serves as a reminder of the overarching vision and the collective effort required to realize it.

To maintain momentum and morale, leaders break

down these long-term goals into smaller, more manageable milestones. Celebrating the achievement of these milestones becomes a key part of the strategy, providing much-needed motivation and recognition of the team's hard work. These celebrations are not just about acknowledging progress but also about reinforcing the team's commitment to the journey ahead.

Furthermore, the cultivation of a culture of accountability is integral to these commitment strategies. Leaders establish clear expectations and foster an environment where every team member is held accountable for their contributions towards the long-term goals. This culture of accountability ensures that each member of the team consistently aligns their actions and decisions with the strategic objectives of the organization, thereby driving collective success.

PRACTICES ENSURING SUSTAINED EFFORT AND PERSEVERANCE

Visionary leaders recognize the importance of empowering leadership at different levels within the organization, fostering a sense of initiative and responsibility toward long-term goals. They understand that leadership is not confined to top management but can be demonstrated at various levels, empowering individuals to drive progress and make meaningful contributions.

To sustain focus and effort toward long-term objectives, leaders implement incentive systems that align with these goals. Such incentives include not only monetary rewards but also non-monetary recognitions, such as career advancement opportunities and acknowledgment programs. These incentives serve as motivation for team members to stay committed and contribute consistently over time.

Understanding the importance of adequate resources and support, leaders ensure that teams working towards long-term objectives have access to the necessary tools and assistance. This provision of resources is crucial for the successful realization of long-term plans and helps in overcoming potential challenges along the way.

Cultivating a growth mindset within the organization is another key strategy. Leaders encourage continuous learning and adaptation, which are vital in navigating the complexities involved in achieving long-term goals. This mindset fosters resilience and an openness to new ideas and approaches.

Feedback loops and mechanisms for continuous improvement are integral to these strategies. Leaders establish platforms where team members can openly discuss challenges, offer suggestions, and contribute to refining strategies. This ongoing process of feedback and improvement ensures that the approach to achieving long-term objectives remains dynamic and effective.

Flexibility and adaptability in approaches are also emphasized by visionary leaders. They recognize that the path to achieving long-term goals may not always be linear and may require adjustments based on changing circumstances and feedback. This flexibility allows the organization to pivot and adapt strategies as necessary, ensuring that they remain on track for achieving their long-term objectives.

MEASURING SUCCESS AND MAKING ADJUSTMENTS

Visionary leaders prioritize the measurement of their strategic plans' success, employing various tools and methods to gauge effectiveness and make necessary adjustments. Central to this evaluative process is the use of metrics and feedback mechanisms, ensuring that the execution of the strategic plan is consistently monitored and improved.

Key Performance Indicators (KPIs) are carefully selected to align closely with strategic objectives. These KPIs offer quantifiable measures of success, providing leaders with clear benchmarks to monitor and evaluate progress.

A balanced scorecard approach is often adopted, allowing for a comprehensive assessment across multiple dimensions of the organization. This approach goes beyond just financial metrics to include evaluations of customer satisfaction, the efficiency of internal processes, and the growth and development of the organization and its members.

Regular review meetings are scheduled to facilitate a thorough assessment of the strategic plan's progress. These meetings are opportunities to delve into performance data, address any challenges encountered, and identify potential areas for improvement.

Additionally, customer feedback and market responses are given significant weight as indicators of the plan's success. This external input offers crucial insights into the effectiveness of strategies, their reception by customers, and the overall impact on the market. This customer-centric approach ensures that the strategic plan remains relevant and responsive to market needs and expectations.

MAKING ADJUSTMENTS BASED ON FEEDBACK AND RESULTS

The most effective leaders champion a responsive and agile approach in executing strategic plans, staying ready to adapt based on feedback and evolving circumstances. This adaptability is key to swiftly addressing market shifts or internal challenges. The strategic plan is not static but a dynamic, evolving document, constantly undergoing iterative improvements. Feedback, a crucial element of this process, is actively sought from across the organization, ensuring a multifaceted perspective on the plan's effectiveness.

In this process, engaging teams organization-wide in providing feedback is fundamental. This inclusive approach guarantees that the evaluation of the plan's effectiveness encompasses diverse viewpoints, enriching the feedback received. This holistic feedback aids in identifying areas needing refinement, ensuring the plan remains relevant and effective.

Moreover, decisions regarding adjustments to the plan are grounded in data. Leaders rely on tangible data and thorough analytics, prioritizing empirical evidence over mere intuition or anecdotal inputs. This data-driven decision-making approach ensures that adjustments are not just reactive but strategic and informed, aligning closely with the organization's goals and the realities of the external environment.

CHAPTER 10
LEAVING YOUR VISIONARY LEGACY

THE JOURNEY of a visionary leader is not just about leading an organization to success; it's about leaving a mark that extends far beyond the confines of the immediate environment. These extraordinary individuals follow through on their ambitious life's work, impacting not only their organizations but also humanity as a whole. This chapter explores the driving forces behind their enduring commitment and the ways they achieve a lasting impact.

THE DRIVE BEHIND VISIONARY LEADERSHIP

At the core of a visionary leader's motivation lies a deeply rooted purpose or mission that transcends conventional business goals. This driving force often embodies a desire to make a positive societal impact, be it through groundbreaking innovation, social change, or philanthropic efforts. This profound sense of purpose is coupled with personal passions and convictions, transforming their work from a mere career into a calling. This deep connection to their work is the wellspring of their perseverance and resilience.

Visionary leaders are dedicated to continuous learning and adaptation. Their approach and thinking are dynamic, allowing them to stay relevant and effective over time. They build and rely on supportive networks of colleagues, mentors, and advisors, drawing not just strategic support but also inspiration and motivation from these relationships. A key element in sustaining their long-term commitment is maintaining focus on the broader impact of their work, measuring success not only in financial terms but also in the positive change they effect.

These trailblazers set ambitious, long-term goals, which act as guiding lights for their efforts and decisions over extended periods. They tackle challenges with innovative problem-solving, often transforming obstacles into opportunities. A significant aspect of their legacy is their ability to inspire and empower others. By nurturing talent and encouraging innovation, they amplify their impact through the successes of those they mentor and lead, extending their influence far beyond their direct actions.

BUILDING ICONIC AND LASTING ENTITIES

Visionary leaders excel in creating iconic and enduring entities. These leaders lay the groundwork with strong core values and a clear purpose that permeate every aspect of their organizations. This foundation guides decisions, operations, and innovations, as seen in companies like Patagonia with its commitment to environmental sustainability.

Innovation and adaptability are prioritized to ensure relevance. Leaders cultivate a culture that embraces new ideas and challenges the status quo, keeping the organization dynamic and forward-looking. Part of building an enduring brand involves developing a strong, distinctive identity, encompassing visual elements, messaging, and the overall experience associated with the brand.

Cultivating customer loyalty is crucial. Leaders like Steve Jobs created products that met and anticipated customer needs, fostering loyalty that spans generations. Investing in quality and excellence ensures that the company's offerings remain top-notch, solidifying its reputation. Strategic long-term planning positions the entity to capitalize on future trends.

A strong internal culture aligned with the entity's values and mission drives employee engagement and productivity—essential for long-term success. Diversifying and evolving over time, leaders adapt to changing market conditions and explore new areas that align with the core mission. A legacy mindset is essential—thinking about the long-term impact and how the entity will continue to thrive beyond their direct involvement.

LEADING INDUSTRY-WIDE CHANGE

Visionary leaders possess the extraordinary ability to initiate changes that extend beyond their organizations, impacting entire industries. Their approaches to driving industry-wide innovation and transformation are multifaceted and influential.

Such leaders often establish new industry standards by innovating and excelling, thereby redefining what's possible and encouraging others in the industry to elevate their practices. Elon Musk's work with Tesla, which expedited the shift of the automotive industry towards electric vehicles, is a prime example of this.

They also focus on creating disruptive technologies and business models that challenge existing norms. These groundbreaking solutions compel industries to evolve, as seen with Amazon's revolutionary e-commerce model that transformed retail by focusing on online shopping and customer experience.

Encouraging open innovation and collaboration is another tactic they employ. By sharing innovations, like patents or research, they not only advance the industry but also position themselves as pivotal figures in its evolution.

Additionally, these leaders engage in championing regulatory and policy changes to support transformation. Recognizing that lasting change often requires shifts in the regulatory landscape, they advocate for these changes, understanding their impact on the industry's future direction.

INSPIRING INNOVATION AND TRANSFORMATION ON A BROADER SCALE

Visionary leaders inspire and influence entire industries through a variety of impactful methods. They often engage in thought leadership, sharing their insights and visions through speaking engagements, publications, and industry forums. This approach inspires others in the industry to embrace new ideas and possibilities.

In addition to thought leadership, these leaders focus on building strategic alliances, including partnerships with competitors. These alliances often work towards shared goals that benefit the whole industry, fostering a collaborative approach to industry-wide change.

Leading by example is another key strategy. Visionary leaders demonstrate the feasibility and benefits of the changes they advocate. Their successful initiatives serve as proof of concept, encouraging others in the industry to adopt similar approaches.

They also play a crucial role in nurturing talent and fostering innovation ecosystems. Recognizing the importance of a skilled professional pool and an environment conducive to ongoing innovation, they invest in these areas to ensure the industry's continuous growth and development.

Moreover, these leaders engage in public advocacy and community engagement, raising awareness and garnering support for their initiatives. This broad engagement amplifies their impact, extending their influence beyond their organizations to shape the industry at large.

CREATING A LASTING IMPACT AND LEGACY

Visionary leaders prioritize the establishment of enduring legacies, embedding their principles and work in ways that continue to influence beyond their direct involvement. A key aspect of this is the institutionalization of core values and principles within their organizations. They embed these values in company policies, cultural norms, and operational strategies, ensuring their longevity beyond their own tenure.

Succession planning is also a vital component of their strategy. These leaders thoughtfully identify and mentor potential successors who resonate with their vision and values. This careful planning ensures a seamless transition and the continuity of their work.

Building self-sustaining organizations is another focus area for visionary leaders. They aim to create entities that can independently grow, adapt, and prosper. This is achieved by establishing robust systems, processes, and a strong culture that fosters ongoing innovation and growth.

Furthermore, they often initiate legacy projects or programs with long-term impacts. These initiatives, closely aligned with the leader's core mission and values, are designed to continue delivering benefits and driving change well after the leader's departure, thereby cementing their lasting impact.

ENSURING CONTINUED INFLUENCE AND INSPIRATION

Visionary leaders often extend their influence beyond their immediate professional sphere by engaging in various impactful activities. Establishing foundations, think tanks, or non-profits is a common strategy. These entities carry on their work in critical areas like research, social change, education, or innovation, sustaining their impact over time.

Another way they leave a lasting mark is through authoring influential works. By writing books or articles or creating content that encapsulates their philosophies and insights, these leaders spread their ideas to broader audiences.

Cultivating a culture of mentorship within their organizations is also pivotal. This practice ensures that the leader's wisdom and experience are imparted to future generations of professionals, thereby amplifying their impact.

These leaders are often involved in educational initiatives as well. Their engagement can take various forms, such as delivering guest lectures, establishing scholarships, or forming partnerships with academic institutions. Such involvement helps inspire and shape future leaders.

Finally, their philanthropic endeavors allow them to make a substantial impact on societal and global issues. This extension of their work into the realm of philanthropy further broadens the scope and significance of their legacy, touching lives and communities beyond their immediate industry or sector.

MENTORING FUTURE INNOVATORS

Visionary leaders recognize the importance of mentoring and nurturing the next generation of innovators and leaders. They understand that their legacy includes imparting their knowledge, experience, and insights to future visionaries, ensuring a continuous flow of innovative leadership and thinking.

Many forward-thinking pioneers engage personally in mentorship, guiding young or less experienced individuals. These one-on-one interactions allow them to share wisdom and experiences and offer tailored guidance, significantly impacting the mentee's personal and professional growth.

They also create robust development opportunities within their organizations. By allowing emerging talent to tackle challenging projects, these leaders provide a platform for future leaders to hone their skills, think creatively, and acquire valuable experience.

Another key approach is fostering a culture that emphasizes continuous learning and growth. By valuing personal and professional development, these leaders ensure that all members of the organization are motivated to realize their potential. This culture often manifests in various forms, including training programs, workshops, and access to diverse learning resources.

Moreover, these innovators encourage an entrepreneurial mindset among their protégés, nurturing qualities like innovation, risk-taking, and resilience. They create environments where experimentation and learning from failures are not only accepted but encouraged, providing a safe space for mentees to develop and thrive. This approach is instrumental in cultivating a new generation of leaders who are equipped to navigate and shape the future.

INFLUENCING THE NEXT GENERATION OF VISIONARIES

Visionary leaders extend their influence and guidance beyond their immediate circle through various means, effectively shaping future innovators and leaders across a wider spectrum.

Leaders generously share their leadership philosophies and insights, not just within their organizations but also through public speaking engagements, written works, and informal discussions. This approach allows them to impart wisdom and lessons learned from their experiences to a broader audience, extending their impact beyond their direct mentees.

They also play a crucial role in networking and community building. By introducing emerging leaders to professional networks and communities, these visionaries provide them with essential connections that can aid in their growth and development. This networking is key in opening doors for opportunities, collaborations, and broader industry exposure.

Participation in academic institutions is another avenue through which these leaders mold future talent. Engaging in activities such as guest lecturing or advising student projects, they bring real-world experience and insights to the academic realm. This involvement allows them to influence aspiring professionals and students, fostering an environment ripe for nurturing future innovation.

Most significantly, visionary leaders lead by example. Their actions, decisions, and the unique paths they carve out become a living curriculum for future leaders. By observing and learning from the way these leaders navigate challenges, make decisions, and drive innovation, emerging leaders gain invaluable lessons that textbooks alone cannot provide. This embodiment of leadership principles in action serves as a powerful and enduring educational tool.

INTEGRATING VALUES AND PRINCIPLES INTO ORGANIZATIONAL DNA

A visionary leader's enduring influence often manifests in the way their values and principles become intertwined with the organization's very essence. These leaders meticulously embed these foundational aspects into the fabric of the organization, shaping its culture, guiding its decision-making, and directing its future trajectory.

The process starts with a clear articulation of the organization's core values and principles. By defining these elements explicitly, leaders ensure that everyone within the organization is not only aware of them but also understands their significance. This step is crucial for setting a solid foundation upon which the rest of the organization can build.

More than just stating these values, visionary leaders weave them into the very practices of the organization. This integration spans various facets, including hiring practices, onboarding processes, day-to-day operations, and decision-making protocols. Such a thorough infusion ensures that these values transcend beyond being mere abstract notions to becoming active, lived experiences within the organizational life.

Leadership modeling plays a pivotal role in this process. Leaders themselves exemplify these values and principles through their actions and decisions. This embodiment of the core values serves as a powerful, tangible example for others within the organization, reinforcing the importance and applicability of these principles.

An organization's commitment to these values is bolstered through regular training and development initiatives. These programs are designed not only to educate employees about the values and principles but also to provide practical insights on how to incorporate them into their daily work and interactions. This ongoing reinforcement helps in firmly rooting these values within the organizational culture, ensuring their longevity and continued relevance.

ENSURING THE PERSISTENCE OF CORE ELEMENTS

Leaders committed to a visionary approach focus intensely on cultivating an organizational culture that naturally mirrors the core values and principles of the entity. This culture becomes a guiding force, influencing behaviors and decisions even without explicit direction, seamlessly integrating these values into the everyday fabric of the organization.

A key strategy in achieving this integration is encouraging active employee involvement in discussions and initiatives that revolve around these values. This approach not only deepens employees' understanding but also strengthens their commitment to these principles. Engaged employees are more inclined to embody and advocate these values, playing a crucial role in their perpetuation.

To ensure enduring adherence to these values, regular evaluations and alignment checks are indispensable. These assessments help maintain the organization's strategic and operational alignment with its foundational elements, ensuring a consistent trajectory that resonates with its core values.

Succession planning is approached with a keen focus on these values. The selection of successors is not just about skills and competencies but also about their alignment with the organization's values and principles. Such an approach guarantees the continuation of these core elements in future leadership, ensuring they remain at the heart of the organization.

Finally, these values and principles are often cemented within the organization's governance structures. By embedding them into boards, committees, and policy documents, they become an integral part of the organization's framework, guiding its operations and shaping its future direction. This institutionalization acts as a safeguard, ensuring that these values continue to influence the organization's trajectory and decisions long into the future.

CONCLUSION: EMBRACING VISIONARY LEADERSHIP

As we reach the conclusion of Leadership Strategy: The Art & Science of Decision-Making, it's crucial to reflect on the key lessons and insights gleaned from the journeys of some of the most transformative leaders of our time. This book has not just been a study of exceptional individuals but a roadmap for anyone aspiring to leave their mark on the world. We now issue a call to action, encouraging you, the reader, to embrace the mantle of visionary leadership in your endeavors.

Throughout our exploration, we uncovered key insights into visionary leadership. We discovered the significance of thinking expansively and challenging established norms to identify transformational opportunities. Visionaries like Elon Musk exemplify the potency of envisioning change on a grand scale and daring to reimagine the conventional.

We've emphasized the indispensable role of courage

and resilience in visionary leadership and covered the importance of taking intelligent risks and persevering in the face of uncertainty, defining these qualities as emblematic of visionary success.

We delved into the concept that visionaries do not merely enhance existing industries but instead revolutionize them. Their adeptness in harnessing technology and fostering creative thinking serves as a catalyst for identifying uncharted opportunities.

Maintaining alignment with a well-defined vision while retaining adaptability emerged as a pivotal strategy. It ensures that futuristic leaders and their organizations remain unwavering in their pursuit of their overarching objectives.

Visionary leaders were portrayed as masterful communicators who can vividly depict a future vision, rally teams around it, and create environments where everyone is deeply committed to the mission.

The book underscored the importance of precise strategy execution and the need for tactical adjustments when required. It emphasized the delicate balance between unwavering determination and adaptability.

Finally, we explored how visionaries guarantee that their principles and contributions endure beyond their own tenure, continuing to inspire and influence long after they have left their mark.

EMBRACE VISIONARY LEADERSHIP

The real-world examples of trailblazing innovators in this book are not just stories of success; they are invitations to action. You are encouraged to embrace these principles in your journey, regardless of your field or position.

Consider the example of Satya Nadella at Microsoft. When Nadella took over as CEO, he not only transformed the company's business strategy but also its culture. He shifted the focus from a 'know-it-all' to a 'learn-it-all' culture, emphasizing empathy, collaboration, and continuous learning. This shift not only rejuvenated Microsoft but also set a new standard in tech leadership. Nadella's approach demonstrates that being a visionary leader is as much about cultivating the right mindset and culture as it is about strategic brilliance.

As you step forward, remember that the path of visionary leadership is not reserved for a select few. It's a path open to anyone willing to embrace change, challenge norms, and lead with purpose. Whether you're leading a team, a company, or just starting your career, you have the potential to be a visionary. The future favors the bold, and it's time for you to reimagine what's possible.

As Steve Jobs once said, "The people who are crazy enough to think they can change the world are the ones who do." Let this be your inspiration as you embark on your journey to reshape industries, disrupt the status quo, and change the world.

Made in the USA
Monee, IL
07 November 2024

69580049R00105